Cybersecurity: from Zero to Hero

MARIA BRYGHT

DEDICATION

To my family, whose unwavering support and encouragement have been my anchor in the tumultuous seas of the cybersecurity realm. Your patience and understanding have not only sustained me but have also been the silent force behind every word written in this book. To you, I dedicate this work, a testament to the power of love and support in overcoming challenges and achieving dreams. Thank you for being my safe harbor.

TABLE OF CONTENTS

ACKNOWLEDGEMENTS

In writing this book on cybersecurity, I have traversed a journey that extended well beyond the confines of my own knowledge and experiences. It is a path that I have not walked alone, and it is with profound gratitude that I acknowledge those who have contributed to the realization of this work.

Firstly, I extend my heartfelt thanks to my academic mentors and colleagues in the cybersecurity community. Your insights and feedback have been invaluable, not only in shaping the content of this book but also in broadening my perspectives on the ever-evolving landscape of cybersecurity.

To the professionals and experts who generously shared their time and knowledge through interviews and discussions, thank you. Your real-world experiences and solutions have added depth and authenticity to the pages of this book, offering readers a practical and insightful view into the world of cybersecurity.

INTRODUCTION

Cybersecurity matters immensely to every business. Protecting our networks from cyber attacks and keeping our customers' private data secure are priorities for us all, emphasizing the need for robust cybersecurity measures. This necessity has sparked a great need for experts skilled in addressing cybersecurity concerns. Join me in navigating the challenges that cybersecurity experts face. This book is crafted for beginners. For those new to cybersecurity, this book offers all the essential information you need to get started. And if you're a tech professional who has some experience with security, this book will assist you in covering any areas you might have missed, ensuring you have a strong base of knowledge.

IMPORTANCE OF CYBERSECURITY

Cybersecurity refers to the practice of protecting computer systems, networks, and data from digital attacks, unauthorized access, or damage. It encompasses a wide range of techniques, technologies, processes, and controls designed to safeguard the integrity, confidentiality, and availability of information technology (IT) systems and data. Cybersecurity is a critical component of both individual and organizational digital health, playing a vital role in securing sensitive information, personal data, intellectual property, and government and industry information systems.

Importance of Cybersecurity

1. Protecting Personal Information: One of the most valuable commodities in the digital age is personal information. If a hacker can steal personal data, they can use it for numerous malicious purposes, including identity theft, financial fraud, or even personal blackmail.

2. Ensuring Business Continuity: For businesses, a significant cybersecurity breach can halt operations, leading to financial losses and damage to brand reputation. Cybersecurity measures are crucial in preventing attacks that can disrupt business activities and ensuring that businesses can continue operations even after a security breach.

3. Safeguarding National Security: On a larger scale, cybersecurity is essential for protecting the data and operational secrecy of national and international institutions, including defense agencies and other critical infrastructure. Cyber attacks on these entities could threaten national security.

4. Compliance with Regulations: Various laws and regulations mandate the protection of data, especially in sectors like healthcare, finance, and public services. Cybersecurity measures are necessary to comply with these regulations, avoiding legal consequences and fines.

5. Protecting Against Ransomware and Malware: Cybersecurity helps in defending against software designed to damage or gain unauthorized access to systems, such as ransomware, viruses, and worms. These malicious programs can encrypt data for ransom, steal information, or cause other harm.

6. Enhancing Customer Trust: In the digital economy, consumer trust is paramount. Companies that demonstrate strong cybersecurity practices can build trust with their customers, assuring them that their data is handled securely and responsibly.

7. Economic Security: Cybersecurity is also crucial for economic security. Cyber attacks can cause economic disruptions, affect stock markets, and lead to significant financial losses for companies and

economies.

8. Preventing Unauthorized Access: Cybersecurity measures help prevent unauthorized access to networks and devices, ensuring that sensitive data and operational capabilities are not compromised.

9. Intellectual Property Protection: For many organizations, intellectual property is a core asset. Cybersecurity protects these assets from theft or espionage, preserving competitive advantage and innovation.

10. Social Stability: On a broader societal level, cybersecurity helps maintain the stability and reliability of digital services that people depend on daily, including financial systems, healthcare records, and communication networks.

WHY START A CAREER IN CYBERSECURITY

Diving into cybersecurity is an exhilarating journey. It's a field brimming with opportunities to acquire new skills and overcome fresh challenges, in an industry that's continuously expanding. While the rewards are plentiful, there are also hurdles to navigate. Let's delve deeper.

The demand for security experts spans far beyond the tech sector alone. Various industries, including healthcare, aviation, finance, transport, nonprofit organizations, and retail, to list just a few, are in need of skilled security personnel. And the demand is substantial. Reports from Forbes and the US Bureau of Labor Statistics indicate that jobs in information security are expected to surge by 33% within this decade, a growth rate four times the average national rate. By 2025, it's estimated that there will be 3.5 million unfilled cybersecurity positions. This opens up immense possibilities for those eager to enter and advance within this domain.

One of the perks of being a security engineer is the potential for salary growth. Although salaries can vary based on factors like experience, employer, and geographic location, the compensation for security professionals is generally high, with the possibility of reaching six figures.

However, entering the security sector isn't without its challenges. A survey by startacybercareer.com highlights some common issues faced by security workers, including being on-call for extended periods, monotonous tasks, and resource shortages. These difficulties can differ by workplace, but the risk of burnout in cybersecurity is genuine. After spending a decade in this field, I can't stress enough the importance of maintaining a work-life balance for longevity in your career. I achieve this by choosing employers who respect my personal time and by setting firm boundaries.

With the right support network and clear goals, a career in cybersecurity can be transformative. Whether you're fresh out of college or contemplating a career shift, I urge you to devise a plan for the next three to six months on how you can make a successful transition into the field.

A PIECE OF HISTORY

The history of cybersecurity traces back to a time before the internet became a cornerstone of daily life, evolving alongside technological advancements to address the growing array of cyber threats.

The Origins:

The concept of cybersecurity originated in the 1970s, following the creation of ARPANET, the precursor to the internet, designed for secure communication between military bases and universities in the United States. The first known instance of a computer virus was the Creeper virus detected on ARPANET in 1971, leading to the creation of the first antivirus software, Reaper, which could find and remove the Creeper virus.

The 1980s: The Rise of Malware

The 1980s saw the rise of personal computing, and with it, the first major computer viruses that spread across PCs. In 1983, Fred Cohen, a PhD student, formally defined a computer virus as "a program that can 'infect' other programs by modifying them to include a, possibly evolved, version of itself." This era also witnessed the emergence of the term "hacker" and the first instances of cyber vandalism.

The 1990s: Internet Expansion and the Birth of Cybersecurity Industry

With the commercialization of the internet in the 1990s, cybersecurity became a significant concern. The proliferation of web browsers and the advent of online commerce platforms introduced new vulnerabilities, leading to the first documented cases of phishing attacks. This period marked the birth of the cybersecurity industry, with companies developing firewalls, antivirus software, and encryption tools to protect data transmission over the internet.

The 2000s: Governmental and Corporate Espionage

The 2000s were characterized by the rise of sophisticated cyber attacks aimed at stealing intellectual property and state secrets. High-profile incidents, such as the infiltration of major corporations and government agencies, underscored the national security implications of cybersecurity. This era also saw the creation of cybersecurity legislation and the formation of dedicated government agencies to combat cyber threats.

The 2010s: The Age of Cyber Warfare and Ransomware

Cybersecurity entered a new phase with the advent of cyber warfare and ransomware attacks. State-sponsored attacks targeting infrastructure, political campaigns, and corporations became commonplace. Ransomware attacks, which encrypt a user's data and demand payment for its release, surged, affecting healthcare systems, municipal governments, and businesses worldwide.

Today and Beyond

Today, cybersecurity is an integral part of national security strategies, corporate risk management, and individual privacy protection. The Internet of Things (IoT) and the advent of AI and machine learning have introduced both new defenses and vulnerabilities. Cybersecurity is now a global concern, with collaboration between nations, corporations, and individuals being paramount to safeguard against increasingly sophisticated threats.

The history of cybersecurity is a testament to the ongoing cat-and-mouse game between cyber defenders and attackers. As technology continues to evolve, so too will the strategies and tools needed to protect the digital world.

THE ESSENTIAL PARTS OF CYBERSECURITY

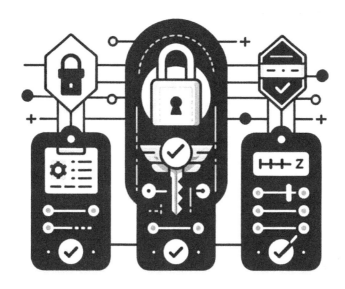

Cybersecurity encompasses a broad range of practices, technologies, and processes designed to protect computers, networks, programs, and data from attack, damage, or unauthorized access. In today's interconnected world, cybersecurity is a critical issue for individuals, businesses, and governments alike. Here are some essential aspects of cybersecurity that are fundamental to understanding and implementing effective security measures.

1. Information Security

At its core, cybersecurity is about protecting information from unauthorized access and breaches. This includes ensuring the confidentiality, integrity, and availability of data. Confidentiality involves keeping sensitive information private, integrity ensures information is accurate and unaltered, and availability means information is accessible to authorized users when needed.

2. Network Security

This aspect focuses on protecting the infrastructure and the networked devices from unauthorized access, misuse, or theft. Network security includes measures such as firewalls, intrusion detection systems (IDS), and virtual private networks (VPNs) to safeguard data being transmitted across networks.

3. Application Security

Application security aims to make software and devices free from threats that might come through flaws in the application design, development, deployment, upgrade, or maintenance. This involves the use of software, hardware, and procedural methods to protect applications from external threats.

4. Operational Security (OpSec)

Operational security includes the processes and decisions for handling and protecting data assets. This encompasses policies for how and where data may be stored or shared and the procedures that determine how access is granted. OpSec also involves the creation of policies that govern how employees use company devices and networks.

5. Disaster Recovery and Business Continuity Planning

Disaster recovery involves restoring IT operations following a cyber-attack, while business continuity planning ensures that critical business functions continue during and after a disaster. Both are essential for minimizing the impact of breaches and attacks on operations.

6. End-User Education

Users often represent the weakest link in cybersecurity. Educating end-users about the dangers of phishing, the importance of strong passwords, and safe internet practices is crucial for bolstering security.

7. Physical Security

Cybersecurity is not just about protecting digital assets but also physical ones. Unauthorized physical access to computers and data centers can compromise an entire network. Physical security measures include surveillance cameras, locks, and security guards.

8. Legal, Regulations, and Compliance

Understanding and adhering to legal requirements and standards is crucial for protecting data and avoiding fines. This includes regulations like GDPR in Europe, HIPAA in the healthcare sector in the United States, and other industry-specific standards.

9. Incident Response

An incident response plan outlines the steps to take when a cyber-attack occurs. This includes identifying the breach, containing the damage, eradicating the cause, recovering systems and data, and learning from the attack to prevent future incidents.

10. Emerging Technologies

Staying ahead of emerging technologies such as artificial intelligence (AI), machine learning, and blockchain is crucial for future-proofing cybersecurity strategies. These technologies can both introduce new vulnerabilities and offer innovative solutions for cybersecurity challenges.

Cybersecurity is a broad field that encompasses various specialized teams, each focusing on different aspects of security to protect organizations from cyber threats. These teams work together to create a robust defense against a wide array of cyberattacks. Understanding the roles and responsibilities of these different teams can provide insight into the complex ecosystem of cybersecurity. Here are some of the key teams involved in cybersecurity:

1. Security Operations Center (SOC) Team

The SOC team is responsible for monitoring, analyzing, and protecting an organization from cyber threats in real-time. They use advanced software tools to continuously scan for anomalies and security breaches, manage security incidents, and ensure that potential threats are identified and mitigated promptly.

2. Incident Response (IR) Team

The IR team is activated when a security breach is detected. Their main responsibility is to manage the response to cyberattacks, containing the threat, eradicating the cause, recovering affected systems, and minimizing damage. They also analyze the incident to improve future response efforts and prevent similar attacks.

3. Threat Intelligence Team

This team focuses on gathering and analyzing information about existing and emerging threats. By understanding the tactics, techniques, and procedures (TTPs) of adversaries, the threat intelligence team helps the organization anticipate, identify, and prepare for potential attacks.

4. Penetration Testing Team

Also known as ethical hackers, the penetration testing team proactively seeks vulnerabilities in an organization's systems and networks by simulating cyberattacks. Their goal is to identify and fix security weaknesses before malicious attackers can exploit them.

5. Compliance and Risk Management Team

This team ensures that the organization complies with all relevant cybersecurity laws, regulations, and standards. They assess and manage the risks associated with the organization's information technology environment, developing policies and procedures to mitigate these risks.

6. Cybersecurity Policy and Strategy Team

Responsible for developing and implementing the overarching cybersecurity strategy and policies, this team ensures that cybersecurity measures align with the organization's objectives and risk appetite. They also keep the organization up to date with evolving cyber laws and regulations.

7. Security Architecture Team

The security architecture team designs and implements the security frameworks that protect the organization's IT infrastructure. They work closely with the IT department to ensure that all systems are built and maintained according to security best practices.

8. End-User Education and Awareness Team

Since human error can lead to significant security vulnerabilities, this team focuses on training and educating employees about cybersecurity best practices, phishing awareness, and safe computing habits to minimize risks.

9. Digital Forensics Team

Following a cybersecurity incident, the digital forensics team investigates what happened by analyzing digital clues. They recover data from damaged or erased devices, analyze malware, and provide evidence for legal cases if necessary.

10. Product Security Team

For organizations that develop software products, the product security team ensures that security is integrated into the product development lifecycle. They assess product designs for vulnerabilities, implement security features, and manage software security updates.

Each of these teams plays a crucial role in the comprehensive defense strategy of an organization, contributing their specialized skills and knowledge to protect against and respond to cyber threats effectively. Collaboration and communication among these teams are essential for a strong and responsive cybersecurity posture.

BLUE TEAM AND RED TEAM

In the realm of cybersecurity, organizations often employ various specialized teams to enhance their security posture and resilience against cyber threats. Among these, the concepts of Blue Team and Red Team are widely recognized, each playing distinct roles in cybersecurity exercises. Additionally, other variants like Purple Teams and White Teams have emerged, offering a more integrated or oversight approach. Here's an overview of each:

Blue Team

The Blue Team consists of an organization's internal security team whose primary role is to defend against both real and simulated cyber threats. They are responsible for maintaining the organization's security posture by implementing and managing security measures, monitoring systems for signs of attack, responding to incidents, and recovering from breaches. The Blue Team's objective is to detect and stop attacks as effectively as possible, ensuring the integrity, confidentiality, and availability of data.

Red Team

The Red Team operates as simulated adversaries, conducting planned attacks on the Blue Team's defenses to test the organization's cybersecurity resilience. They use techniques and strategies that real attackers might employ to find vulnerabilities, including social engineering, system exploitation, and penetration testing. The purpose of the Red Team is to challenge the Blue Team's defenses, identify weaknesses, and provide feedback for improving security measures.

Purple Team

The Purple Team is not a separate entity but rather a concept that represents the collaboration between Red and Blue Teams. The idea is to maximize the effectiveness of both teams by ensuring direct communication, sharing insights, and learning from each exercise. Purple Team exercises help in translating the findings of Red Team attacks into actionable defense strategies for the Blue Team, fostering a continuous improvement loop in cybersecurity practices.

White Team

The White Team typically oversees and manages cybersecurity exercises between the Red and Blue Teams. They set the rules of engagement, objectives, and scope for these exercises, ensuring that both teams stay within predefined boundaries. The White Team also acts as arbitrators, evaluating the performance of both teams, providing feedback, and ensuring that lessons learned are documented and applied. In some contexts, the White Team may also be involved in broader cybersecurity governance, policy-making, and compliance roles.

Green Team

Although less commonly mentioned, the Green Team focuses on the day-to-day IT operations and development within an organization, working closely with the Blue Team to implement secure technologies and practices. They play a critical role in ensuring that security recommendations are practical, sustainable, and integrated into the organization's technology environment.

Black Team

In some cybersecurity discussions, a Black Team may refer to external attackers or real-life adversaries whose motivations and actions are unknown and not controlled by the organization. The concept of the Black Team serves as a reminder of the constant, unpredictable threat that organizations face, driving the need for continuous vigilance and improvement in cybersecurity measures.

Each of these teams, whether actual or conceptual, plays a vital role in strengthening an organization's cybersecurity framework. By simulating attacks, defending against them, and learning from each encounter, organizations can better prepare themselves against the ever-evolving landscape of cyber threats.

THE CYBER KILL CHAIN

In the 1990s, cyber attacks were mostly associated with pranks by teenagers exploring their hacking abilities for amusement. However, the opportunity for criminal activities via the Internet was quickly realized, along with the potential for using online connectivity for espionage. Today, cyber attacks are predominantly executed by organized crime groups and government-backed operatives employing systematic approaches. In 2009, Lockheed Martin's Cyber Emergency Response Team developed a pivotal research paper titled "Intelligence-Driven Computer Network Defense Informed by Analysis of Adversary Campaigns and Intrusion Kill Chains," available for download on their website. This paper introduced what's widely recognized today as the Cyber Kill Chain, detailing an attack in seven stages: Reconnaissance, Weaponization, Delivery, Exploitation, Installation, Command and Control, and Action. An attack may not strictly follow this sequence, as stages often overlap, but each phase marks a critical point in executing the attack.

Reconnaissance involves identifying a target and learning its attributes, akin to scoping out a location. Typically, individuals have a single internet address assigned by their Internet Service Provider, while a business may have multiple addresses under their internet domain. An attack against a business often begins with a known website address, followed by scanning nearby internet spaces for other systems linked to the target, known as an IP address scan. Once active hosts are identified, the attacker examines each to discover accessible entry points, a process called a Port scan, to find potential attack vectors and the software versions they run. Modern attacks are seldom manual; attackers usually rent time on a network of compromised computers, or Botnets, to perform automated scans, enabling large-scale cyber attacks.

Weaponization involves tailoring a known vulnerability to specific targets, integrating it into an automated attack platform. The weaponized malware might be designed to exploit a certain operating system or a specific online service. Nowadays, with hacking seen as a service, cybercriminals often buy weaponized malware from specialized developers instead of creating their own. The most common malware delivery methods include email attachments, compromised websites inviting the target for a visit, or using stolen credentials to implant malware directly. An attack might need to establish a foothold on an internet-facing host to reach deeper targets not directly connected to the internet. Sometimes, malware is delivered via an infected flash drive, exploiting software vulnerabilities when the device is used.

Post-delivery, an infected file or website exploits software vulnerabilities, or stolen credentials are used for direct system entry. Following exploitation, the attacker or malware moves to take action, which might involve installing a payload for persistent access or immediate action. Malware installation often ensures the payload restarts with the system, such as by modifying Windows registry entries. Once installed, the malware typically contacts a Command and Control server, signaling a compromised host, ready for further instructions. Actions taken by the malware depend on the attacker's motives, ranging from website defacement by hacktivists, data theft by state-sponsored agents, to financial theft by cybercriminals. Regardless of the motive, the outcome is seldom beneficial for the target.

Reflect on recent cyber incidents in the news. While the final action of an attack might be reported, the delivery methods are less discussed. Considering the Cyber Kill Chain can provide insight into the unseen phases of these attacks.

THE EVOLUTION OF CYBER THREATS

The digital landscape has undergone profound transformations since the advent of computers, and with it, the nature of cyber threats has evolved. Understanding this evolution is crucial for grasping the complexities of modern cybersecurity challenges. This chapter delves into the historical progression of cyber threats, highlighting key moments and shifts that have shaped the threat landscape.

The Early Days

The genesis of cyber threats can be traced back to the early days of computing, even before the internet became a household name. Initially, viruses and malware were primarily created by hobbyists and programmers to demonstrate technical prowess or for sheer curiosity. The 1980s saw the emergence of the first significant viruses that spread through floppy disks, demonstrating the potential for malicious software to disrupt computer operations.

The Internet Era

With the commercialization of the internet in the 1990s, the cyber threat landscape began to change dramatically. The connectivity that the internet provided also opened up new avenues for attackers. The infamous Morris Worm of 1988 was among the first to exploit network vulnerabilities, causing significant disruption and highlighting the need for cybersecurity measures.

The Rise of Cybercrime

As the internet grew in popularity, it became a fertile ground for criminal activities. The late 1990s and early 2000s saw an increase in financially motivated attacks, including phishing scams, credit card fraud, and identity theft. This period marked the transition of cyber threats from mere annoyances to serious criminal enterprises.

State-Sponsored Cyber Espionage

The 2000s also witnessed the emergence of state-sponsored cyber espionage, where governments leveraged cyber capabilities to spy on other nations, steal intellectual property, and even sabotage critical infrastructure. Incidents like Stuxnet, which targeted Iranian nuclear facilities, underscored the potential for cyber attacks to have real-world geopolitical implications.

The Age of Ransomware and Advanced Persistent Threats (APTs)

In recent years, the cyber threat landscape has been dominated by ransomware attacks and APTs. Ransomware, which encrypts victims' data and demands payment for its release, has affected millions of individuals and organizations, causing billions in damages. APTs, characterized by their stealth and persistence, aim to infiltrate networks for extended periods to steal information or conduct espionage, often backed by nation-states.

The Future of Cyber Threats

As technology continues to advance, so too do cyber threats. The proliferation of Internet of Things (IoT) devices, the advent of artificial intelligence (AI), and the increasing reliance on cloud services all present new challenges and attack vectors. Cybercriminals are becoming more sophisticated, employing machine learning and automation to enhance the efficacy of their attacks.

The evolution of cyber threats reflects the broader technological and societal changes of the past decades. From simple viruses to complex state-sponsored cyber operations, the escalation in the severity and sophistication of these threats necessitates a robust and adaptive cybersecurity posture. Understanding this evolution is not just an academic exercise; it's a critical step in anticipating and defending against the cyber threats of tomorrow.

By the end of the 1990s, online commerce had emerged as a vital component of the global economy, catching the attention of organized crime for its potential for high rewards at low risk through the internet. As a result, cybercrime saw a rapid increase, particularly in the theft of credit card information from databases, marking a significant threat for companies. This threat materialized as data breaches, which posed severe risks to businesses, especially with the payment card industry imposing fines for failing to meet cybersecurity standards. By 2010, the scale of cybercrime had matched that of the illegal drug trade. Recent years have witnessed numerous major data breaches, including significant incidents involving the

Shanghai Police, Syniverse, and Facebook, with Facebook experiencing a breach of half a billion records, marking one of the largest in recent times. However, credit cards aren't the only sensitive data at risk. In June 2015, the US government acknowledged the theft of personnel files and security clearance information of more than 4 million current and former employees. While governments have long been targets of cyber attacks, attributing these attacks to their sources has often been challenging. For instance, in June 2007, the Pentagon suffered what was then described as the most successful cyber attack against the US Defense Department, with the US pointing fingers at China. This attack was part of a series known as Titan Rain, though China denied any involvement. The first publicly acknowledged act of cyber sabotage occurred in 2010 when the US and Israel were reported to have developed and deployed Stuxnet malware against Iran's nuclear program, effectively hindering its nuclear capabilities. More recently, cyber influence campaigns, such as the one targeting Clinton's emails to interfere with the election process, represent a new type of threat.

Explore the extensive records of the world's largest data breaches, and take a moment to investigate smaller incidents, like the data loss faced by the craft beer company BrewDog, to grasp the extensive reach of cyber threats.

BASIC CYBERSECURITY TERMINOLOGY

Understanding the language of cybersecurity is crucial for navigating and comprehending the vast landscape of cyber threats and defense mechanisms. This chapter introduces basic cybersecurity terminology, laying the foundation for deeper exploration into the field. Here, we break down essential terms and concepts that form the backbone of cybersecurity discussions.

Malware

Malware, short for malicious software, refers to any software intentionally designed to cause damage to a computer, server, client, or computer network. Examples include viruses, worms, trojans, and ransomware.

Virus

A Virus is a type of malware that, when executed, replicates itself by modifying other computer programs and inserting its own code. It often spreads to other computers through email attachments or compromised software.

Worm

A Worm is a standalone malware computer program that replicates itself in order to spread to other computers. Unlike a virus, it does not need to attach itself to an existing program and often exploits network vulnerabilities to spread.

Trojan Horse

A Trojan Horse, or Trojan, is any malware which misleads users of its true intent. It often disguises itself as legitimate software. Trojans can be used by cyber-thieves and hackers trying to gain access to users' systems.

Ransomware

Ransomware is a type of malicious software designed to block access to a computer system until a sum of money is paid. It typically encrypts files, making them inaccessible, and demands a ransom for the decryption key.

Phishing

Phishing is the fraudulent attempt to obtain sensitive information such as usernames, passwords, and credit card details by disguising oneself as a trustworthy entity in an electronic communication.

Firewall

A Firewall is a network security device that monitors incoming and outgoing network traffic and decides whether to allow or block specific traffic based on a defined set of security rules.

Encryption

Encryption is the process of converting information or data into a code, especially to prevent unauthorized access. It is a crucial tool for protecting data privacy and securing communications.

VPN

A VPN, or Virtual Private Network, extends a private network across a public network, enabling users to send and receive data across shared or public networks as if their computing devices were directly connected to the private network.

Two-Factor Authentication (2FA)

Two-Factor Authentication adds an additional layer of security to the process of authentication by requiring two different forms of identification before granting access to an account or system.

Cyber Espionage

Cyber Espionage involves the use of computer networks to gain illicit access to confidential information, typically held by a government or other organization, for strategic, military, or competitive advantage.

Botnet

A Botnet is a network of private computers infected with malicious software and controlled as a group without the owners' knowledge, e.g., to send spam messages or launch attacks.

Zero-Day Exploit

A Zero-Day Exploit targets a previously unknown vulnerability in a computer application or operating system, meaning the developers have "zero days" to fix the flaw because it was previously unknown.

Patch

A Patch is a piece of software designed to update a computer program or its supporting data, to fix or improve it. This includes fixing security vulnerabilities and other bugs.

This glossary of basic cybersecurity terminology is by no means exhaustive but offers a primer to the language and concepts that are frequently encountered in the field of cybersecurity. Understanding these terms is the first step toward building a solid foundation in cybersecurity knowledge.

CONFIDENTIALITY, INTEGRITY, AND AVAILABILITY (CIA TRIAD)

The CIA Triad stands as the cornerstone of cybersecurity, embodying the primary objectives that inform the protection of information systems. This foundational concept includes Confidentiality, Integrity, and Availability, each serving as a critical pillar in the architecture of secure information systems. Understanding the CIA Triad is essential for anyone venturing into the field of cybersecurity, as it provides a framework for evaluating and implementing security measures.

Confidentiality

Confidentiality concerns the protection of sensitive information from unauthorized access and disclosure. It ensures that data is accessible only to those with the requisite authorization, safeguarding personal privacy and proprietary information. Techniques for maintaining confidentiality include data encryption, stringent access controls, and rigorous authentication processes. By encrypting data, even if unauthorized access is gained, the information remains unintelligible and useless to the intruder. Confidentiality breaches can lead to significant financial losses, legal repercussions, and damage to an organization's reputation.

Integrity

Integrity refers to the assurance that information is trustworthy and accurate, and has not been tampered with or altered by unauthorized individuals. Maintaining data integrity is crucial for the reliability of information systems, as any unauthorized alteration can lead to misinformation, impacting decision-making processes and operational functionality. Methods to uphold integrity include checksums, cryptographic hash functions, and digital signatures, which verify that data has remained unchanged from its source. Regular audits and monitoring are also vital for detecting and mitigating integrity breaches.

Availability

Availability ensures that information and resources are accessible to authorized users when needed. This aspect of the CIA Triad addresses the readiness of systems, highlighting the importance of operational continuity even in the face of attacks or technical failures. Strategies to enhance availability include redundant systems, regular software updates, and robust disaster recovery plans. Denial of Service (DoS) attacks, which aim to overwhelm systems and render them unusable, are direct threats to availability. Thus, safeguarding against such disruptions is paramount for maintaining business operations and service delivery.

Balancing the Triad

Achieving a balance among confidentiality, integrity, and availability is a challenging yet critical aspect of cybersecurity. Overemphasizing one element of the triad can lead to vulnerabilities in another. For instance, overly restrictive access controls (confidentiality) might hinder the availability of data for legitimate use. Similarly, ensuring high availability through multiple redundancies might inadvertently create more targets for potential breaches, affecting confidentiality.

The CIA Triad in Practice

Implementing the principles of the CIA Triad requires a holistic approach to cybersecurity, involving a combination of technological solutions, policies, and user education. For example, organizations must deploy firewalls and intrusion detection systems while also fostering a security-aware culture among employees. Regular training and awareness programs can significantly reduce the risk of breaches by informing users about phishing scams, the importance of strong passwords, and the proper handling of sensitive data.

The CIA Triad is a fundamental concept that underpins the field of cybersecurity. By understanding and applying the principles of confidentiality, integrity, and availability, cybersecurity professionals can develop comprehensive strategies to protect information systems against an ever-evolving array of threats. This triad serves not only as a theoretical framework but as a practical guide for implementing effective security measures, ensuring the safeguarding of digital assets in an increasingly connected world.

THE CONCEPT OF DEFENSE IN DEPTH

In the complex and ever-evolving landscape of cybersecurity, relying on a single layer of defense is insufficient to protect against the myriad of threats that organizations face. This reality has given rise to the concept of Defense in Depth (DiD), a strategy that employs multiple layers of security controls and measures spread throughout an information system. Originating from a military strategy that aims to delay rather than prevent the advance of an attacker, Defense in Depth in cybersecurity seeks to ensure that if one defensive layer fails, others will continue to provide protection.

Principles of Defense in Depth

Defense in Depth is built on the premise that no single security measure is infallible; each layer of security may have potential vulnerabilities that can be exploited by determined attackers. The DiD approach addresses this issue by creating a multifaceted defense system where each layer serves a specific purpose and complements the others, thereby increasing the overall security posture of an organization.

Layers of Defense

Physical Security: The first line of defense involves physical measures to protect the hardware and infrastructure that store and process data. This includes secure locks, surveillance cameras, access control systems, and environmental controls against fire or flooding.

Network Security: This layer focuses on protecting the network from unauthorized access and threats. Firewalls, intrusion detection systems (IDS), intrusion prevention systems (IPS), and secure network architecture are key components.

Endpoint Security: Securing the devices that connect to the network, such as computers, smartphones, and tablets, is crucial. Solutions include antivirus software, anti-malware tools, and personal firewalls.

Application Security: This involves securing applications from threats by implementing secure coding practices, regular vulnerability scanning, and patch management. Application firewalls and encryption also play a role.

Data Security: Protecting the data itself, regardless of where it resides or moves, through encryption, data masking, and secure storage solutions ensures confidentiality and integrity.

Identity and Access Management (IAM): Controlling who has access to resources and ensuring they are who they claim to be is fundamental. This is achieved through authentication, authorization, and auditing mechanisms.

Policies, Procedures, and Awareness: The human element cannot be overlooked. Educating employees about cybersecurity best practices, phishing, and social engineering attacks is vital. Clear security policies and procedures guide behavior and response to incidents.

Benefits of Defense in Depth

The primary benefit of implementing a Defense in Depth strategy is the significant reduction in risk exposure. By layering defenses, an organization can protect against a broader range of threats, from physical breaches to sophisticated cyber attacks. Additionally, DiD provides redundancy; if one layer fails, others stand in defense, reducing the likelihood of a successful breach. It also offers the flexibility to adjust and evolve security measures as new threats emerge.

Challenges and Considerations

While Defense in Depth is a powerful security strategy, it is not without challenges. Managing multiple layers of security can be complex and resource-intensive. There is also the risk of creating a false sense of security if not properly implemented or maintained. Therefore, organizations must carefully plan and continuously evaluate their DiD strategy to ensure it effectively addresses current and future security needs.

Defense in Depth is a comprehensive approach to cybersecurity that acknowledges the multifaceted nature of threats. By implementing layered security measures across the physical, network, endpoint, application, data, and human aspects of an organization, Defense in Depth provides a robust framework for protecting information systems. It emphasizes not just the prevention of attacks but also the resilience and recovery of systems, making it a critical strategy in the fight against cyber threats.

RISK MANAGEMENT IN CYBERSECURITY

Risk management is an integral component of a comprehensive cybersecurity strategy. It involves the identification, analysis, evaluation, and mitigation of risks associated with cyber threats to an organization's information and systems. Effective risk management ensures that cybersecurity measures are aligned with the organization's objectives and tolerance for risk, thereby protecting assets while optimizing resource allocation.

Understanding Cyber Risks

Cyber risks are potential threats that could exploit vulnerabilities in an organization's systems or processes, leading to unauthorized access, data breaches, loss of data integrity, or service disruptions. These risks arise from a variety of sources, including external attackers, insider threats, software flaws, and operational weaknesses. The first step in managing these risks is to understand and categorize them based on their potential impact and likelihood.

The Risk Management Process

Risk Identification: The process begins with identifying potential cyber threats and vulnerabilities that could harm the organization. This involves conducting regular security assessments, vulnerability scanning, and threat intelligence gathering.

Risk Analysis: Once risks are identified, they are analyzed to understand their potential impact on the organization and the likelihood of their occurrence. This analysis considers both qualitative and quantitative factors, such as financial impact, reputational damage, and regulatory implications.

Risk Evaluation: Based on the analysis, risks are evaluated

against the organization's risk tolerance levels to determine their acceptability. This step prioritizes risks, helping decision-makers understand which ones require immediate attention and resources for mitigation.

Risk Mitigation: For risks deemed unacceptable, appropriate mitigation strategies are developed and implemented. Mitigation options may include avoiding the risk, transferring it (e.g., through insurance), mitigating it through security controls, or accepting it if it falls within the organization's risk tolerance.

Monitoring and Review: Cybersecurity is dynamic, with new threats emerging constantly. Therefore, the risk management process is ongoing, requiring regular monitoring of the threat landscape and review of risk assessments and mitigation measures to ensure they remain effective.

Key Concepts in Cyber Risk Management

Asset Valuation: Understanding the value of the assets being protected is crucial for determining the level of security investment required.

Threat Modeling: This involves systematically identifying and assessing potential attackers, their goals, and the methods they might use to breach security.

Vulnerability Assessment: Regularly assessing the vulnerabilities within an organization's systems and processes helps in identifying areas of weakness that need strengthening.

Incident Response Planning: Having a plan in place for responding to cybersecurity incidents minimizes their impact and aids in swift recovery.

Challenges in Cyber Risk Management

Managing cyber risks presents several challenges, including the rapidly evolving nature of cyber threats, the complexity of information systems, and the difficulty in quantifying certain types of risk. Additionally, the human factor often introduces unpredictability into cybersecurity efforts.

Strategic Risk Management

Effective cyber risk management requires a strategic approach that aligns with the organization's overall objectives and risk appetite. It involves not only the IT department but also senior management and other key stakeholders across the organization. By fostering a culture of risk awareness and incorporating cybersecurity into strategic planning, organizations can better navigate the cybersecurity landscape.

Risk management in cybersecurity is about making informed decisions to protect an organization from the potential adverse effects of cyber threats. By systematically identifying, analyzing, evaluating, and mitigating risks, organizations can enhance their resilience against cyber attacks. Continual monitoring and review ensure that the risk management strategy adapts to new threats and changes in the organization's risk tolerance, keeping its information and assets secure in a constantly evolving cyber environment.

TYPES OF CYBER THREATS

MALWARE: VIRUSES, WORMS, AND TROJANS

Malware, short for malicious software, encompasses various forms of harmful software designed to disrupt, damage, or gain unauthorized access to computer systems. Among the most prevalent types of malware are viruses, worms, and Trojans, each with unique characteristics and methods of propagation. Understanding these malicious entities is crucial for developing effective cybersecurity defenses.

Viruses

A virus is a type of malware that attaches itself to clean files and infects a computer system without the user's knowledge. It requires human action to propagate, such as opening an infected email attachment or downloading and executing a malicious file. Once activated, viruses can replicate and spread to other files, potentially corrupting system functionality, erasing data, or stealing information. Antivirus software and cautious behavior online are key to preventing virus infections.

Key Characteristics:

- Requires user interaction to spread.
- Attaches to executable files.
- Capable of self-replication and payload delivery.
- Prevention Tips:
- Use updated antivirus software.
- Avoid opening attachments or links from unknown sources.
- Keep your operating system and software updated.

Worms

Worms are malware similar to viruses, but they can propagate independently without human interaction. Utilizing network vulnerabilities or exploiting software flaws, worms spread across networks, replicating themselves on any connected system they can reach. This autonomous spreading capability can lead to widespread damage, including overwhelming network resources, stealing sensitive data, or installing backdoors for future attacks. Defending against worms involves maintaining network security and patching software vulnerabilities promptly.

Key Characteristics:

- Spreads autonomously without human action.
- Exploits network vulnerabilities.
- Can cause widespread network disruption.
- Prevention Tips:
- Implement firewalls and intrusion detection systems.
- Regularly update and patch systems and software.
- Isolate infected systems to prevent spread.

Trojans

A Trojan or Trojan horse, in contrast to viruses and worms, disguises itself as legitimate software. Users are tricked into installing Trojans, believing them to be genuine applications. Once installed, Trojans can perform a variety of malicious actions, such as creating backdoors, capturing keystrokes (keylogging), or joining the computer to a botnet. Unlike viruses and worms, Trojans do not replicate but rely on social engineering to spread. Vigilance and reputable antivirus solutions are crucial for detecting and removing Trojans.

Key Characteristics:

- Disguised as legitimate software.
- Does not self-replicate.
- Performs malicious actions stealthily.
- Prevention Tips:
- Download software from trusted sources only.
- Use comprehensive security software with Trojan detection.
- Be wary of too-good-to-be-true offers that could be Trojan lures.

Viruses, worms, and Trojans represent significant threats in the cybersecurity landscape, each with distinct propagation methods and impacts. Understanding these threats is the first step toward safeguarding computer systems and networks. Implementing robust security measures, practicing safe browsing habits, and staying informed about emerging malware trends are essential strategies for defense against these malicious entities.

PHISHING AND SOCIAL ENGINEERING ATTACKS

In the vast domain of cybersecurity threats, phishing and social engineering attacks stand out for their reliance on manipulating human psychology rather than exploiting technical vulnerabilities. These types of attacks are designed to trick individuals into divulging sensitive information or performing actions that compromise security. Understanding the mechanics and varieties of these attacks is crucial for defending against them.

Phishing: The Art of Deception

Phishing attacks involve sending fraudulent communications

that appear to come from a reputable source, typically via email, but also through text messages (smishing) or voice calls (vishing). The goal is to steal sensitive data like login credentials, credit card numbers, or install malware on the victim's device. Phishing messages often create a sense of urgency, prompting the recipient to act quickly without scrutinizing the legitimacy of the request.

Key Characteristics:

- Masquerades as legitimate communications.
- Aims to steal sensitive information or deliver malware.
- Creates a sense of urgency to prompt immediate action.

Prevention Tips:

- Verify the sender's information before responding to unexpected requests.
- Avoid clicking on links or downloading attachments from unknown or suspicious emails.
- Use email filtering solutions and keep security software updated.

Spear Phishing: Targeted Deception

Spear phishing is a more sophisticated form of phishing that targets specific individuals or organizations. Attackers spend time gathering information about their targets to create highly personalized messages, making the fraudulent communication more convincing. Spear phishing is particularly dangerous because of its tailored approach, which increases the likelihood of the targeted individual complying with the malicious request.

Key Characteristics:

- Highly personalized to the target.
- Involves detailed research on the victim.
- More difficult to detect due to its customized nature.

Prevention Tips:

- Be cautious of unsolicited emails that request sensitive information, even if they seem to know you.
- Implement two-factor authentication on sensitive accounts to add an extra layer of security.
- Conduct regular security awareness training that includes information on identifying spear phishing attempts.

Social Engineering: Beyond Phishing

Social engineering attacks encompass a broader range of tactics beyond phishing, aiming to exploit human psychology to bypass security measures. These attacks can occur online or offline, involving pretexting (fabricating scenarios to steal information), baiting (offering something enticing to deliver malware), or tailgating (unauthorized physical entry by following authorized personnel). Social engineering is predicated on building trust with the victim or exploiting their natural curiosity or fear.

Key Characteristics:

- Exploits human psychology rather than technical flaws.
- Can occur in both digital and physical realms.
- Relies on building trust or exploiting emotions.

Prevention Tips:

- Educate employees about the various forms of social engineering and encourage a culture of security.
- Implement strict policies for verifying identity before providing access to sensitive information or areas.
- Encourage skepticism and verification before acting on unusual requests.

Phishing and social engineering attacks are formidable because they target the human element of cybersecurity. Awareness and education are the most effective defenses against these deceptive tactics. By fostering an environment where security is a shared responsibility, and by implementing technical safeguards and policies, individuals and organizations can significantly reduce their vulnerability to these insidious attacks.

Ransomware: What It Is and How to Protect Against It

Ransomware represents one of the most direct and financially damaging cyber threats faced by individuals and organizations worldwide. This type of malware encrypts the victim's files or locks them out of their system, demanding a ransom payment for the decryption key or system access. Understanding ransomware's nature, its impact, and protective measures is crucial for cybersecurity resilience.

Understanding Ransomware

Ransomware attacks involve malicious software that encrypts files on a device or network, rendering them inaccessible to the user. Victims are typically notified via a message on their screen, explaining that their data has been encrypted and demanding a ransom, usually in cryptocurrency, for the decryption key. The anonymity of cryptocurrencies like Bitcoin makes tracking and prosecuting the perpetrators challenging, emboldening attackers and fueling the ransomware economy.

The Impact of Ransomware

The consequences of a ransomware attack can be severe, ranging from temporary loss of access to critical data to complete operational shutdowns. For businesses, the impact extends beyond the ransom payment, encompassing data recovery costs, reputational damage, and potential legal liabilities for compromised customer data. The psychological toll on victims, both individuals, and organizations, can also be significant, fostering a climate of fear and urgency that may lead to hasty decisions.

Protecting Against Ransomware

Protection against ransomware requires a multifaceted approach, incorporating both preventative measures and preparedness for potential attacks.

Regular Backups: Maintain regular, secure, and redundant backups of critical data. Backups should be stored offline or in a separate environment to prevent them from being encrypted by ransomware.

Timely Updates and Patching: Keep all systems, software, and applications updated to protect against vulnerabilities that could be exploited by ransomware.

Security Software: Use reputable antivirus and anti-malware solutions with real-time protection capabilities. Advanced endpoint protection platforms can detect and block ransomware attacks before they encrypt data.

Email Security: Implement email filtering and scanning solutions to detect and block phishing emails, a common vector for ransomware distribution.

Access Controls: Apply the principle of least privilege to all systems and services, ensuring users have only the access necessary for their roles.

Employee Awareness Training: Educate employees about the risks of ransomware and phishing tactics used to distribute malicious software. Training should emphasize the importance of not clicking on suspicious links or attachments.

Incident Response Plan: Develop and regularly update an

incident response plan that includes specific procedures for responding to ransomware attacks. Knowing how to quickly isolate infected systems can limit the spread of the malware.

Avoid Paying the Ransom: Paying the ransom does not guarantee decryption of files and may encourage further attacks. Instead, focus on prevention, preparation, and collaboration with law enforcement.

Ransomware poses a significant threat in the digital age, capable of crippling organizations and causing distress to individuals. However, by understanding the threat, implementing robust security practices, and fostering a culture of cybersecurity awareness, it is possible to mitigate the risk and impact of ransomware attacks. Preparation, education, and resilience are key to navigating the challenges posed by this formidable cyber threat.

INSIDER THREATS AND HOW THEY OPERATE

In the complex ecosystem of cybersecurity threats, insider threats occupy a unique and particularly challenging position. Unlike external attacks that originate from outside the organization, insider threats come from within—carried out by individuals who have legitimate access to the organization's networks, systems, and data. Understanding how insider threats operate and the motives behind them is crucial for developing effective strategies to mitigate these risks.

Defining Insider Threats

Insider threats can be intentional or unintentional actions by employees, contractors, or business associates that compromise the security, confidentiality, integrity, or availability of the organization's information or information systems. These threats can range from malicious insiders deliberately stealing, sabotaging, or leaking data for personal gain or to harm the organization, to well-meaning individuals who inadvertently cause security breaches through negligence or lack of awareness.

How Insider Threats Operate

Insider threats are particularly insidious for several reasons:

Legitimate Access: Insiders have authorized access to the organization's systems and sensitive data, bypassing many of the external defenses like firewalls and intrusion detection systems.

Knowledge of the Organization: They have knowledge of the organization's policies, procedures, and potential vulnerabilities, which they can exploit to carry out their activities without detection.

Difficult to Detect: The legitimate access and knowledge insiders possess make their malicious activities harder to detect using conventional security tools and techniques.

Motivations Behind Insider Threats

Understanding the motivations behind insider threats is key to preventing them. These motivations can include:

Financial Gain: The desire for personal financial benefit is a common motivator, with insiders selling sensitive information to competitors or engaging in fraud.

Ideology: Disgruntled employees may leak information to harm the organization due to disagreements with its policies or practices.

Espionage: Insiders may spy on behalf of foreign governments or entities, particularly in industries related to national security, defense, or high-tech innovation.

Accidental: Often, insiders do not intend harm but inadvertently cause security breaches through careless actions, such as falling for phishing scams, misconfiguring systems, or mishandling data.

Mitigating Insider Threats

Mitigating insider threats requires a comprehensive approach that includes both technological solutions and organizational strategies:

User Activity Monitoring: Implement tools that can detect unusual access patterns or data movement that may indicate malicious insider activity.

Least Privilege Access: Limit access rights for users to the minimum necessary for them to perform their job functions.

Data Loss Prevention (DLP) Technologies: Use DLP tools to monitor and control data transfers, preventing unauthorized data exfiltration.

Regular Audits: Conduct regular audits of system and data access to identify potential insider threat activities.

Security Awareness Training: Educate employees about the risks of insider threats and encourage a culture of security awareness and responsibility.

Employee Support Programs: Provide support for employees who may be facing personal or professional challenges, reducing the risk of disgruntlement leading to malicious activities.

Insider threats pose a significant risk to organizations, capable of causing extensive damage due to the perpetrators' access and knowledge. Tackling these threats requires a blend of proactive and reactive strategies, focusing on minimizing opportunities for insider malfeasance while promoting a strong culture of security awareness and ethical conduct. By understanding how insider threats operate and implementing robust security measures, organizations can better protect themselves against the dangers lurking within.

CYBERSECURITY TECHNOLOGIES

FIREWALLS AND THEIR ROLE IN NETWORK SECURITY

In the realm of cybersecurity, firewalls serve as a critical first line of defense, safeguarding information systems from unauthorized access and various cyber threats. Acting as gatekeepers between secure internal networks and potentially unsecured external networks, such as the internet, firewalls play an indispensable role in network security. This chapter delves into the nature of firewalls, their operational mechanisms, and their significance in maintaining the security integrity of networks.

The Essence of Firewalls

A firewall is a network security device or software that monitors and controls incoming and outgoing network traffic based on predetermined security rules. Essentially, it establishes a barrier between a trusted internal network and untrusted external networks to block malicious traffic, such as hackers, viruses, and worms, from accessing and compromising the network.

Types of Firewalls

Packet Filtering Firewalls: These are the most basic form of firewalls that make decisions based on the source and destination addresses, ports, or protocols. They examine each packet's header and either allow or block it according to the set rules.

Stateful Inspection Firewalls: Going beyond packet filtering, stateful firewalls monitor the state of active connections and make decisions based on the context of the traffic, allowing for more granular control.

Proxy Firewalls (Application-Level Gateways): Acting as an intermediary between users and the internet, proxy firewalls evaluate requests at the application layer. They provide in-depth inspection and can block specific content or websites.

Next-Generation Firewalls (NGFW): These combine the capabilities of traditional firewalls with advanced features like application awareness and control, integrated intrusion prevention, and cloud-delivered threat intelligence. NGFWs provide a deeper inspection based on the application's identity, not just the port or protocol.

Key Functions of Firewalls

Access Control: Firewalls enforce access control policies, determining which services and resources can be accessed by internal and external users.

Traffic Monitoring: They monitor network traffic to detect and prevent unauthorized access, cyber attacks, and malware dissemination.

Intrusion Prevention: By inspecting traffic for known attack signatures or anomalous patterns, firewalls can identify and block potential threats.

VPN Support: Many firewalls support Virtual Private Network (VPN) connections, allowing secure remote access to the network.

Implementing Firewalls for Network Security

The effective deployment of firewalls involves several critical considerations:

Placement: Proper placement is essential, with firewalls typically positioned between any external connection and the network perimeter.

Configuration: Firewalls must be carefully configured with specific rules tailored to the organization's network security policy.

Regular Updates and Maintenance: To remain effective against new threats, firewall rules and firmware should be regularly updated and audited.

Challenges and Best Practices

While firewalls are indispensable, they are not infallible. Cyber threats are constantly evolving, necessitating vigilant management of firewall configurations. Best practices include:

Minimizing Complexity: Simplify firewall rules to avoid conflicts and ensure they are understandable and manageable.

Regular Auditing: Periodically review and audit firewall rules and configurations to ensure they align with current security policies.

Layered Defense: Employ a layered security approach (Defense in Depth) that includes additional security measures beyond firewalls, such as intrusion detection systems (IDS), antivirus software, and security information and event management (SIEM) solutions.

Firewalls are foundational to network security, providing a critical barrier against a wide range of cyber threats. By understanding the different types of firewalls, their operational mechanisms, and best practices for deployment, organizations can significantly enhance their network security posture. As part of a comprehensive security strategy, firewalls mitigate the risk of cyber attacks and maintain the integrity and confidentiality of networked systems.

INTRUSION DETECTION AND PREVENTION SYSTEMS (IDPS)

Intrusion Detection and Prevention Systems (IDPS) are pivotal components in the cybersecurity defense mechanisms of modern networks. They not only detect malicious activities and policy violations but also play a crucial role in preventing such activities from causing harm. This chapter explores the fundamentals of IDPS, their operational mechanisms, and their indispensable role in bolstering network security.

Understanding IDPS

IDPS are technologies that monitor networks and systems for malicious activity or policy violations. When such activities are detected, the IDPS responds by alerting security administrators and, in the case of intrusion prevention systems, taking action to block or prevent the malicious activity. These systems are essential for identifying and mitigating threats in real-time, thereby enhancing the overall security posture of an organization.

Types of IDPS

Network-Based IDPS (NIDPS): These systems monitor network traffic for suspicious activity. They are typically deployed at strategic points within the network to monitor inbound and outbound traffic for signs of attacks.

Host-Based IDPS (HIDPS): Unlike NIDPS, HIDPS are installed on individual hosts or devices. They monitor the inbound and outbound traffic from the device, as well as system configurations and application activity, to detect potential security breaches.

Signature-Based Detection: This method relies on known patterns of malicious activity, called signatures, to identify threats. While effective against known threats, it may not detect new, unknown attacks.

Anomaly-Based Detection: Anomaly-based detection uses machine learning to establish a baseline of normal network behavior. It alerts administrators of any deviations from this baseline, which could indicate a potential threat.

Behavior-Based Detection: Similar to anomaly-based detection, behavior-based detection focuses on understanding the behavior of applications or users to identify malicious activities.

Operational Mechanisms of IDPS

Detection: IDPS continuously monitor network traffic or system activities for signs of malicious behavior or policy violations. This involves analyzing data packets, monitoring system logs, and scrutinizing user behaviors.

Alerting: Upon detecting suspicious activity, IDPS generate alerts to notify security personnel. These alerts typically include detailed information about the incident to aid in response efforts.

Prevention: Intrusion prevention systems take a step further by actively blocking or mitigating the identified threat. This can include terminating malicious processes, blocking IP addresses, or reconfiguring network devices.

Challenges and Considerations

While IDPS are powerful tools in detecting and preventing intrusions, they come with their own set of challenges. False positives, where benign activities are mistakenly identified as malicious, can lead to unnecessary alerts, potentially overwhelming security teams. Conversely, false negatives, where malicious activities go undetected, can leave organizations vulnerable to attacks. Balancing sensitivity to detect threats without generating excessive false positives is a critical consideration for IDPS effectiveness.

Best Practices for IDPS Deployment

Strategic Placement: For NIDPS, strategic placement at the network perimeter and critical internal junctions maximizes visibility into traffic flows. HIDPS should be installed on critical servers and endpoint devices.

Regular Updates: Keeping IDPS signatures and algorithms up to date is vital for detecting the latest threats.

Tuning and Customization: IDPS should be tuned and customized to the specific environment to minimize false positives while maximizing detection capabilities.

Integration with Other Security Tools: Integrating IDPS with other security tools, such as SIEM systems and firewalls, can provide a more comprehensive security posture.

Intrusion Detection and Prevention Systems are cornerstone technologies in the cybersecurity arsenal, offering critical capabilities to detect, alert, and prevent malicious activities and policy violations. By understanding the types, mechanisms, and best practices associated with IDPS, organizations can significantly enhance their ability to safeguard against a wide array of cyber threats, maintaining the integrity, confidentiality, and availability of their information systems.

ANTIVIRUS SOFTWARE AND ANTI-MALWARE TOOLS

In the battleground of cybersecurity, antivirus software and anti-malware tools play a pivotal role in defending digital environments from the plethora of threats that aim to infiltrate, damage, or hijack systems and data. These defense mechanisms are sophisticated software solutions designed to detect, neutralize, and eliminate malicious software, or malware, thereby safeguarding computing resources and sensitive information. This chapter delves into the essentials of antivirus and anti-malware tools, their operational dynamics, and the significance of their application in maintaining robust cybersecurity.

Fundamentals of Antivirus and Anti-Malware Protection

Antivirus software and anti-malware tools are crafted to combat the wide array of malware, including viruses, worms, trojans, ransomware, spyware, adware, and more. While 'antivirus' historically referred to tools designed specifically against computer viruses, the modern use of the term and the functionality of such software have expanded to offer comprehensive protection against various forms of malware.

Key Mechanisms of Action

Signature-Based Detection: One of the oldest and most common detection methods, this approach involves identifying malware based on a database of known malware signatures—distinctive strings of data or characteristic code sequences used to identify specific malware instances. Regular updates are crucial for the effectiveness of signature-based detection, as they ensure the software can recognize the latest threats.

Heuristic Analysis: This technique enables antivirus programs to detect new, previously unknown viruses or variants of existing viruses by analyzing code for suspicious characteristics. It is especially useful for identifying malware for which a signature is not yet available.

Behavioral Detection: Also known as behavior-based or anomaly detection, this approach monitors the behavior of programs and applications to identify actions that might indicate malicious intent, such as unauthorized data transmission or unexpected system changes.

Sandboxing: Some advanced anti-malware tools use sandboxing to run and analyze suspicious programs in a controlled, isolated environment. This prevents potentially harmful programs from interacting with the real system, allowing safe observation of their behavior.

The Crucial Role of Antivirus and Anti-Malware Tools

Proactive Protection: By continuously monitoring and scanning systems for signs of malware, these tools offer proactive protection against the installation or execution of malicious software.

Threat Identification and Removal: Upon detecting a threat, antivirus and anti-malware tools can quarantine or delete the malicious software, mitigating potential damage.

System Integrity and Performance: Regular scans help maintain system integrity and performance by removing malware that can slow down or disrupt system operations.

User Confidence: Effective antivirus and anti-malware protection boosts confidence among users, knowing their systems and data are safeguarded against cyber threats.

Best Practices for Effective Use

Regular Updates: Ensure your antivirus and anti-malware software is regularly updated to recognize the latest threats.

Comprehensive Scans: Schedule regular, comprehensive scans of your system to detect and remove any lurking malware.

Smart Browsing and Download Habits: Complement your software's protection with smart browsing habits and cautious downloading practices to minimize the risk of malware infection.

Multi-Layered Security Approach: Employ a multi-layered security approach that includes firewalls, secure networks, and vigilant email practices alongside antivirus and anti-malware tools for comprehensive protection.

Antivirus software and anti-malware tools are indispensable allies in the ongoing battle against cyber threats. Their sophisticated detection and remediation capabilities are crucial for securing digital assets against the ever-evolving landscape of malware. By understanding their mechanisms and implementing best practices for their use, individuals and organizations can significantly bolster their cybersecurity defenses.

ENCRYPTION: SECURING YOUR DATA

In the digital era, where data breaches and cyber threats loom large, encryption stands as a fortress in the realm of cybersecurity. This critical technology transforms readable data into a coded form, ensuring that only authorized parties can access the original information. This chapter delves into the principles of encryption, its types, and its pivotal role in safeguarding personal and corporate data against unauthorized access.

The Essence of Encryption

Encryption is the process of converting plaintext into ciphertext—a scrambled, unreadable format—using an algorithm and an encryption key. This cryptographic method ensures data confidentiality and security, whether the data is at rest (stored data) or in transit (data being transferred over networks). The process is reversible only with the appropriate decryption key, allowing the intended recipient to convert the ciphertext back to its original plaintext form.

Types of Encryption

Symmetric Encryption: This type involves a single key that both encrypts and decrypts the data. It's fast and efficient for large volumes of data but requires secure key exchange mechanisms to ensure the key's confidentiality.

Asymmetric Encryption: Also known as public-key encryption, it uses two keys: a public key for encryption and a private key for decryption. The public key can be shared openly, while the private key is kept secret by the owner, facilitating secure communications between parties without the need for a secure key exchange.

Hashing: Though not an encryption method in the traditional sense, hashing converts data into a fixed-size string of characters, which represents the data's fingerprint. Hash functions are designed to be one-way, meaning the original data cannot be retrieved from the hash value, ensuring data integrity.

Applications of Encryption

Secure Communications: Encryption is vital for protecting sensitive communications, such as emails, messaging services, and online transactions, ensuring that only the intended recipients can access the information.

Data Protection: Encrypting data stored on devices or in the cloud protects against unauthorized access, making it essential for safeguarding personal information, intellectual property, and corporate secrets.

Digital Signatures: Asymmetric encryption facilitates digital signatures, which verify the authenticity of digital documents and the identity of the signatory, bolstering trust in electronic transactions.

Compliance: Encryption helps organizations comply with data protection regulations, such as the General Data Protection Regulation (GDPR) and the Health Insurance Portability and Accountability Act (HIPAA), which mandate the protection of sensitive data.

Best Practices for Implementing Encryption

Strong Encryption Standards: Utilize strong, widely accepted encryption standards and algorithms, such as AES (Advanced Encryption Standard) for symmetric encryption and RSA or ECC (Elliptic Curve Cryptography) for asymmetric encryption.

Key Management: Implement robust key management practices, including secure generation, storage, exchange, and periodic rotation of keys to mitigate the risk of compromise.

Encrypt by Default: Adopt a policy of encrypting data by default, both at rest and in transit, to ensure comprehensive protection across all data touchpoints.

Regular Audits and Updates: Conduct regular audits of encryption practices and stay updated on the latest cryptographic standards and vulnerabilities to maintain the effectiveness of encryption measures.

Encryption is a cornerstone of modern cybersecurity strategies, providing a robust layer of protection for data against unauthorized access and cyber threats. By understanding the principles of encryption and implementing best practices, individuals and organizations can significantly enhance the security of their digital assets. In a world increasingly reliant on digital information, encryption acts as a critical safeguard, ensuring the confidentiality, integrity, and availability of data.

CREATING AND MANAGING STRONG PASSWORDS

In the digital age, the significance of strong passwords cannot be overstated. Passwords act as the first line of defense against unauthorized access to personal and corporate data. Yet, the increasing sophistication of cyber-attacks has made password security more critical than ever. This chapter explores the principles of creating and managing strong passwords, offering guidance on fortifying this essential security barrier.

The Importance of Strong Passwords

A strong password serves as a robust barrier, deterring attackers from gaining unauthorized access to online accounts, sensitive data, and IT systems. Weak passwords, conversely, are easily exploited by cybercriminals using brute-force attacks, dictionary attacks, or social engineering tactics. The strength of a password significantly impacts an individual's or organization's vulnerability to cyber threats.

Principles of Creating Strong Passwords

Length and Complexity: A strong password should be at least 12 characters long, incorporating a mix of uppercase letters, lowercase letters, numbers, and special characters. The complexity and length of a password make it exponentially harder for attackers to crack.

Unpredictability: Avoid using easily guessable information, such as names, birthdays, or common words. Instead, opt for random combinations of characters or use passphrase methods, stringing together unrelated words.

Uniqueness: Use a unique password for each account or service. This prevents a single compromised password from granting an attacker access to other accounts.

Best Practices for Managing Passwords

Password Managers: Considering the difficulty of remembering multiple complex passwords, employing a reputable password manager is highly recommended. Password managers securely store and encrypt passwords, requiring the user to remember only one master password.

Two-Factor Authentication (2FA): Whenever possible, enable two-factor authentication for an added layer of security. 2FA requires a second form of verification, such as a text message code or biometric scan, in addition to the password.

Regular Updates: Change passwords regularly, especially if there's suspicion of a breach. However, avoid excessively frequent changes that might lead to weaker password choices due to fatigue.

Secure Recovery Methods: Ensure that password recovery options are secure. Use strong security questions whose answers cannot be easily guessed or found online, and ensure recovery emails or phone numbers are up-to-date.

Avoiding Common Pitfalls

Avoiding Common Patterns: Patterns like sequential numbers, repeated characters, or keyboard patterns (e.g., "qwerty") are easily predictable.

Resisting Social Engineering: Be cautious of phishing attempts designed to trick users into divulging their passwords. Always verify the authenticity of requests for sensitive information.

Beware of Public Wi-Fi: Avoid entering passwords when connected to unsecured public Wi-Fi networks, as these can be monitored by attackers.

Strong passwords are foundational to cybersecurity, yet creating and managing them effectively presents challenges in a world of countless online accounts and persistent threats. By adhering to the principles of strong password creation and employing best practices for password management, individuals and organizations can significantly enhance their security posture. Remember, in the vast digital landscape, a strong password is not just a key to your digital life; it's a guardian of your digital safety.

Understanding and Using Two-Factor Authentication

As digital threats evolve and become more sophisticated, relying solely on strong passwords for account security is no longer sufficient. Two-factor authentication (2FA) has emerged as a critical layer of protection, adding an extra step to the verification process and significantly enhancing security. This chapter explores the concept of two-factor authentication, its importance, and how to effectively implement and use it.

The Basics of Two-Factor Authentication

Two-factor authentication, also known as dual-factor authentication or 2-step verification, is a security mechanism that requires two distinct forms of identification from users to grant access to an account or system. This method combines something you know (like a password) with something you have (such as a mobile device) or something you are (like a fingerprint). By requiring two different authentication factors, 2FA makes unauthorized access to accounts much more difficult for potential attackers.

Why Two-Factor Authentication Matters

Enhanced Security: Even if a password is compromised, unauthorized users cannot gain access without the second factor, significantly reducing the risk of account breaches.

Reduction of Identity Theft: 2FA provides an additional verification layer that helps protect sensitive personal and financial information from identity theft.

Compliance and Trust: Many industries now require 2FA for compliance with data protection regulations. Implementing 2FA can also build trust with customers by demonstrating a commitment to security.

Types of Two-Factor Authentication

Something You Have: This type includes devices or objects the user possesses, such as security tokens, mobile phones (receiving SMS codes or using authentication apps), or smart cards.

Something You Know: Apart from the password, this could involve an additional PIN, an answer to a security question, or a specific keystroke pattern.

Something You Are: Biometric verification methods fall into this category, including fingerprint scans, facial recognition, iris scans, or voice identification.

Implementing and Using Two-Factor Authentication

Choosing the Right 2FA Method: Evaluate the security needs, convenience, and resource availability of your organization or personal use to select the most suitable 2FA method.

Educating Users: For organizations, it's crucial to train employees on the importance of 2FA and guide them through the setup and daily use of the authentication system.

Regularly Update Security Settings: Keep the 2FA settings and related applications up to date to ensure the highest level of security against new threats.

Best Practices for Two-Factor Authentication

Use Authenticator Apps When Possible: Authenticator apps are generally more secure than SMS codes, which can be intercepted. Apps like Google Authenticator or Authy generate time-based one-time passwords (TOTPs) that change every 30 seconds.

Backup Your 2FA Methods: Ensure you have backup access methods in case your primary 2FA device is lost or unavailable. Many services offer backup codes, which should be stored securely.

Be Cautious of Phishing Attempts: Even with 2FA enabled, be vigilant for phishing attacks designed to trick you into providing your second factor, such as a code or biometric data.

Two-factor authentication is a powerful tool in the cybersecurity arsenal, offering an additional layer of defense that significantly enhances account security. By understanding and implementing 2FA across personal and professional digital spaces, users can protect themselves against the increasing risks of unauthorized access and cyber threats. As part of a comprehensive security strategy, 2FA not only secures data and systems but also fosters a culture of security mindfulness among users.

RECOGNIZING AND AVOIDING PHISHING ATTEMPTS

Phishing is a prevalent cyber threat where attackers deceive individuals into revealing sensitive information, such as passwords, credit card numbers, or personal identification details, by masquerading as a trustworthy entity in digital communications. This chapter explores the hallmarks of phishing attempts, strategies to recognize them, and measures to avoid falling victim to these malicious endeavors.

Understanding Phishing

Phishing attacks are typically carried out through email, but can also occur via text messages (smishing), phone calls (vishing), or social media. Attackers lure victims with seemingly legitimate requests or alarming notifications, urging immediate action that involves submitting personal information or clicking on malicious links. The consequences can range from financial loss to identity theft and significant breaches of corporate security.

Characteristics of Phishing Attempts

Urgency: Phishing messages often create a sense of urgency, pressuring recipients to act quickly without verifying the legitimacy of the request.

Suspicious Links: Links in phishing emails may appear legitimate at first glance but usually direct users to fraudulent websites. Hovering over a link can reveal the actual URL, which often differs from the displayed link text.

Unexpected Requests: Unsolicited requests for sensitive information or unexpected attachments are common red flags.

Typos and Inconsistencies: Phishing attempts may contain spelling errors, grammatical mistakes, or inconsistencies in email addresses, links, and formatting.

Strategies to Recognize Phishing Attempts

Scrutinize the Sender: Verify the sender's email address for any discrepancies. Attackers might use addresses that resemble the legitimate ones with minor alterations.

Examine the Content: Be wary of emails that solicit personal information, convey a sense of urgency, or use generic greetings. Legitimate organizations typically have specific protocols for communication and will not ask for sensitive information via email.

Verify Before Clicking: Avoid clicking on links or downloading attachments from unknown or suspicious sources. Use official websites by typing the URL directly into the browser instead.

Check for Secure Websites: Ensure that any website you visit from an email is secure by looking for "https://" in the URL and the padlock symbol in the browser's address bar.

Measures to Avoid Phishing Attempts

Use Spam Filters: Activate spam filters to minimize the number of phishing emails that reach your inbox.

Employ Security Software: Utilize comprehensive security software that offers email scanning and web protection to detect and block phishing attempts.

Update Regularly: Keep your operating system, browsers, and security software updated to protect against the latest threats.

Educate and Train: For organizations, conducting regular

training sessions to educate employees about phishing and other social engineering attacks is crucial for reinforcing vigilance.

Two-Factor Authentication (2FA): Implementing 2FA adds an additional layer of security, reducing the risk associated with compromised credentials.

Phishing remains one of the most insidious threats in the cybersecurity landscape, leveraging deception to exploit human vulnerabilities. Recognizing the signs of phishing and adopting proactive measures to avoid these attempts are essential skills in the digital age. By staying informed, scrutinizing communications, and employing security best practices, individuals and organizations can significantly mitigate the risk of falling prey to phishing attacks.

SECURE WEB BROWSING AND EMAIL PRACTICES

In the interconnected realm of the internet, secure web browsing and email practices are fundamental to safeguarding personal and organizational data from cyber threats. This chapter outlines essential strategies for navigating the web and managing email communication securely, minimizing the risk of encountering malware, phishing attempts, and other online hazards.

The Pillars of Secure Web Browsing

Use of HTTPS: Always ensure that the websites you visit are secured with HTTPS, indicated by the padlock icon next to the URL. HTTPS encrypts the data transmitted between your browser and the website, protecting it from interception.

Update Your Browser: Regularly updating your web browser ensures that you have the latest security features and patches for known vulnerabilities. Cybercriminals often exploit outdated software to launch attacks.

Utilize Privacy Settings: Adjust your browser's privacy settings to control cookies, JavaScript execution, and access to your webcam and microphone. These settings can help protect your privacy and reduce the risk of malicious scripts running without your consent.

Install Ad-Blockers and Security Extensions: Use reputable ad-blocking and security extensions to prevent malicious ads and pop-ups that might contain malware from loading on your browser.

Be Wary of Public Wi-Fi: When using public Wi-Fi networks, avoid accessing sensitive information or conducting financial transactions, as these networks can be easily compromised. Consider using a virtual private network (VPN) for an added layer of security.

Email Security Practices

Recognize Phishing Emails: Stay vigilant for emails with suspicious links, urgent requests for personal information, or offers that seem too good to be true. Always verify the sender's email address and look for any signs of phishing.

Use Strong, Unique Passwords: Employ strong, unique passwords for your email accounts and change them regularly. Consider using a password manager to securely store your passwords.

Enable Two-Factor Authentication (2FA): Activate 2FA for your email accounts to add an additional security layer, making it more difficult for attackers to gain unauthorized access.

Be Cautious with Attachments and Links: Do not open email attachments or click on links from unknown or untrusted sources. These can be vehicles for malware or phishing sites.

Regularly Update Your Email Client: Whether you use a web-based email service or a standalone email client, ensure it is regularly updated to benefit from the latest security enhancements.

Best Practices for Both Web Browsing and Email

Back Up Your Data: Regularly back up important data to an external drive or cloud storage. In the event of a malware attack, having backups ensures that you don't lose critical information.

Educate Yourself and Others: Stay informed about the latest cybersecurity threats and share this knowledge with friends, family, and colleagues. Awareness is a powerful tool against cybercrime.

Report Suspicious Activity: If you encounter suspicious activity or believe you've fallen victim to a cyberattack, report it to the appropriate authorities or your organization's IT department.

Secure web browsing and email practices are critical components of online safety. By adhering to the guidelines outlined in this chapter, users can significantly reduce their exposure to cyber threats and protect their sensitive information from unauthorized access. Remaining vigilant, continuously educating oneself about emerging threats, and adopting a proactive approach to cybersecurity can help navigate the digital world with confidence.

BASICS OF HOME AND OFFICE NETWORKS

In today's interconnected world, both home and office environments rely heavily on networks to facilitate communication, access information, and perform numerous tasks. Understanding the basics of these networks is crucial for optimizing their performance, ensuring security, and troubleshooting common issues. This chapter explores the foundational elements of home and office networks, highlighting key components, network types, and essential security practices.

Understanding Network Basics

A network consists of two or more computers or devices connected together to share resources, exchange files, or communicate with each other. Networks can range from simple setups in a home to complex configurations in large organizations.

Components of a Network:

Router: Acts as the central hub in most home and office networks, directing traffic between devices and to the internet.

Switch: Used in larger networks to connect multiple devices on the same network within a building or campus.

Modem: Connects a network to the internet, translating between the digital data of a computer and the analog signal of a telephone line or cable system.

Access Points: Extend the wireless coverage of a network, providing Wi-Fi connectivity to devices.

Types of Networks:

Local Area Network (LAN): A network confined to a small area, such as a home, office, or building. LANs typically use wired connections for speed and security.

Wide Area Network (WAN): Covers a large geographical area and connects multiple LANs. The internet is the largest WAN.

Wireless Local Area Network (WLAN): A LAN based on Wi-Fi wireless network technology.

Virtual Private Network (VPN): Extends a private network

across a public network, enabling users to send and receive data as if their computing devices were directly connected to the private network.

Setting Up a Secure Network

Securing your home or office network is paramount to protect sensitive information from unauthorized access and cyber threats.

Change Default Credentials: Default usernames and passwords on routers and other network devices are well-known to attackers. Change these to something secure as soon as you set up your network.

Enable WPA3 Encryption: For wireless networks, ensure that WPA3 encryption is enabled to protect the data transmitted over the network.

Set Up a Guest Network: For businesses and even homes expecting visitors, setting up a separate Wi-Fi network for guests can protect your main network's integrity.

Disable WPS: Wi-Fi Protected Setup (WPS) offers a simplified way to connect devices but can be a security risk. Disable this feature if possible.

Regular Updates: Keep your router's firmware and all network-connected devices updated to protect against known vulnerabilities.

Use Firewalls and Antivirus Software: Ensure that firewalls are enabled on your router and that all connected devices have up-to-date antivirus software to detect and prevent malicious activities.

Educate Users: In office settings, educating employees about safe internet practices and the importance of network security can significantly reduce risks.

Troubleshooting Common Network Issues

Connectivity Problems: Check cables, restart your router and modem, and ensure your device's wireless settings are correctly configured.

Slow Speeds: Limit the number of devices connected, check for interference, and consider upgrading your internet plan or network hardware for better performance.

Security Breaches: Regularly monitor your network for unauthorized access, change passwords immediately if a breach is suspected, and consider a network security audit.

The basics of home and office networks lay the foundation for creating efficient, secure, and reliable connections. By understanding the components, types, and best practices for network setup and maintenance, individuals and organizations can enhance their productivity and safeguard their digital assets against potential threats. Regular maintenance, adherence to security protocols, and staying informed about the latest in network technology and threats are key to managing a successful and secure network.

SECURING WIRELESS NETWORKS

Wireless networks have become ubiquitous in both home and office environments, offering convenience and flexibility that wired networks cannot match. However, this convenience comes with increased vulnerability to security threats. Without proper security measures, wireless networks can be exploited by unauthorized users and cybercriminals. This chapter focuses on the essentials of securing wireless networks, outlining effective strategies to protect against unauthorized access and ensure the confidentiality, integrity, and availability of data transmitted over these networks.

Understanding Wireless Network Vulnerabilities

Wireless networks are inherently more exposed to security threats than wired networks due to their broadcast nature. Signals transmitted over the air can be intercepted by unauthorized users within range, leading to potential data breaches, eavesdropping, or unauthorized network access. Common vulnerabilities include weak encryption, poor access control, and the use of default network settings.

Key Measures for Securing Wireless Networks

Change Default Administrator Passwords: Default usernames and passwords for wireless routers and access points are well-known and easily found online. Changing these to strong, unique credentials is a critical first step in securing your wireless network.

Enable Strong Encryption: Use the most robust encryption protocol available on your wireless network equipment. Currently, WPA3 (Wi-Fi Protected Access 3) offers the highest level of security. If WPA3 is not available, WPA2 should be used.

Disable WPS (Wi-Fi Protected Setup): WPS offers a simplified way to connect devices to your wireless network but can be a security risk due to vulnerabilities in the WPS PIN method. Disable WPS on your router to enhance security.

Use a Strong Wi-Fi Network Password: Create a strong, unique password for your Wi-Fi network to prevent unauthorized access. Avoid common words and include a mix of letters, numbers, and special characters.

Enable Network Name (SSID) Hiding: Hiding your network's SSID (Service Set Identifier) makes it less visible to casual scanners. While not a foolproof security measure, it can help deter less sophisticated threats.

Implement MAC Address Filtering: Although not invulnerable to spoofing, MAC address filtering adds an extra layer of security by allowing only specified devices to connect to your wireless network.

Regularly Update Firmware: Keep your router's firmware up to date to ensure you have the latest security patches and features. Manufacturers often release firmware updates in response to discovered vulnerabilities.

Create a Guest Network: If you often have visitors needing internet access, set up a separate guest network. This keeps your primary network secure while providing internet access to guests.

Limit Wireless Signal Range: Adjust the power settings of your wireless router to limit your network's signal range. This minimizes the chances of outsiders accessing your wireless network from remote locations.

Monitor Network Activity: Regularly check your network for unauthorized devices and unusual activity. Many routers offer logs and tools to help you monitor connections and data traffic.

Securing wireless networks is a dynamic process that requires vigilance and regular maintenance. By implementing the measures outlined in this chapter, users can significantly enhance the security of their wireless networks, protecting sensitive information from unauthorized access and cyber threats. Remember, the goal is to create a balance between convenience and security, ensuring that your wireless network provides the benefits of mobility and flexibility without compromising on safety.

VPNs and Their Importance for Privacy

In an era where digital privacy concerns are escalating, Virtual Private Networks (VPNs) have emerged as essential tools for enhancing online security and privacy. VPNs create a secure and encrypted connection over a less secure network, such as the internet, shielding users' data from prying eyes. This chapter delves into the workings of VPNs, their importance for maintaining privacy, and considerations for their use.

What is a VPN?

A Virtual Private Network (VPN) is a technology that allows you to create a secure connection over a public network. VPNs encrypt your internet traffic and disguise your online identity, making it more difficult for third parties to track your activities online and steal data. The encryption takes place in real time and encompasses all data transmitted during the VPN session.

How VPNs Enhance Privacy

Encryption: VPNs use strong encryption protocols to secure data transmissions, ensuring that even if intercepted, the data remains unreadable to unauthorized users.

Anonymizing IP Addresses: By routing your internet traffic through a VPN server, your actual IP address is masked, making it appear as though the traffic originates from the server's IP address. This helps protect your location and browsing habits from being tracked.

Secure Public Wi-Fi Use: Public Wi-Fi networks are notoriously insecure. VPNs encrypt your data even on public networks, protecting it from being intercepted by cybercriminals.

Bypassing Geo-restrictions: VPNs can also be used to access content restricted to certain regions by connecting to servers in different countries, although this use is subject to legal and ethical considerations.

Choosing the Right VPN

Not all VPNs offer the same level of security and privacy. When choosing a VPN service, consider the following:

Reputation: Opt for a VPN provider with a strong reputation for privacy and security. Research and read reviews from trusted sources.

No-logging Policy: Ensure the VPN provider has a strict no-logging policy, meaning they do not keep records of your internet activities.

Security Features: Look for VPNs that offer strong encryption protocols, kill switches (which automatically disconnect you from the internet if the VPN fails), and DNS leak protection.

Jurisdiction: Consider where the VPN service is based, as this can affect the company's legal obligations regarding data retention and law enforcement requests.

Potential Limitations and Considerations

While VPNs are powerful tools for privacy, they are not without limitations:

Speed and Performance: Encryption and routing traffic through VPN servers can sometimes slow down internet speeds or affect performance.

False Sense of Security: VPNs protect your internet traffic but are not a panacea for all privacy issues. Users should adopt a comprehensive approach to online privacy, including secure passwords and cautious sharing of personal information.

Legal and Ethical Use: Misuse of VPNs for illegal activities can have serious consequences. It is essential to use VPNs ethically and comply with applicable laws and terms of service.

VPNs play a critical role in safeguarding online privacy in an increasingly surveilled and data-driven world. By encrypting data and anonymizing internet activity, VPNs offer a significant layer of protection against cyber threats and privacy intrusions. However, choosing the right VPN provider and understanding the limitations of VPN technology are crucial steps to effectively leveraging VPNs for enhanced privacy. As part of a broader privacy strategy, the judicious use of VPNs can help secure your digital footprint against unwelcome scrutiny.

SECURING PERSONAL DEVICES: COMPUTERS, SMARTPHONES, AND TABLETS

In the contemporary digital landscape, personal devices such as computers, smartphones, and tablets are integral to daily life. However, these devices are also prime targets for cyber threats, including malware, phishing attacks, and unauthorized data access. Ensuring the security of these devices is paramount to protecting personal information, sensitive data, and maintaining privacy. This chapter outlines essential strategies for securing personal devices against cyber threats.

Understanding the Risks

Personal devices face a myriad of security risks, from malicious software that can steal data or encrypt files for ransom, to hackers exploiting vulnerabilities for unauthorized access. Even seemingly benign apps can sometimes harvest data without consent. Recognizing these risks is the first step towards effective device security.

General Security Measures

Regular Updates: Keep your device's operating system and all applications up to date. Manufacturers and developers release updates to patch vulnerabilities and enhance security features.

Antivirus and Anti-Malware Software: Install reputable antivirus and anti-malware software to protect against malicious threats. Ensure it's set to update automatically and perform regular scans.

Secure Wi-Fi Connections: Use secure, password-protected Wi-Fi networks. Avoid conducting sensitive transactions on public Wi-Fi networks, or use a VPN for added security.

Enable Firewalls: Activate built-in firewalls on your devices to monitor and control incoming and outgoing network traffic based on predetermined security rules.

Strategies for Computers

Use Strong Passwords and Authentication: Employ strong, unique passwords for all accounts and enable two-factor authentication where available. Consider using a password manager to securely store passwords.

Backup Data: Regularly backup important data to an external hard drive or cloud storage. This can be crucial for recovery in case of data loss or ransomware attacks.

Encrypt Sensitive Data: Use encryption tools to secure sensitive files and folders, especially if your computer contains personally identifiable information or confidential documents.

Strategies for Smartphones and Tablets

Screen Locks: Implement a strong screen lock, such as a PIN, pattern, or biometric authentication, to prevent unauthorized access if your device is lost or stolen.

App Permissions: Carefully review and manage app permissions to ensure apps only have access to necessary data and features.

Find My Device: Enable 'Find My Device' (iOS) or 'Find My Phone' (Android) services to locate, lock, or erase your device remotely if it's lost or stolen.

Avoid Jailbreaking or Rooting: Jailbreaking or rooting your device can expose it to additional security risks. Stick to official app stores for downloads to reduce the risk of installing malicious apps.

Securing personal devices is an ongoing process that requires vigilance, regular maintenance, and a proactive approach to privacy and security. By implementing the strategies outlined in this chapter, users can significantly enhance the security of their computers, smartphones, and tablets, protecting themselves against the evolving landscape of cyber threats. Remember, the security of your devices not only protects your personal information but also contributes to the overall safety of the digital ecosystem.

SOCIAL MEDIA SECURITY

In an era where social media platforms have become central to personal and professional life, securing one's social media presence is imperative. The ubiquity of these platforms has made them attractive targets for cybercriminals looking to exploit personal information, spread malware, or engage in identity theft. This chapter provides essential guidelines for enhancing social media security and safeguarding against potential threats.

Recognizing Social Media Risks

Social media platforms can pose several security risks, including but not limited to:

Privacy breaches: Inadvertently sharing too much personal information can lead to privacy invasions or identity theft.

Phishing scams: Cybercriminals often use fake profiles or messages to trick users into divulging sensitive information.

Malware distribution: Malicious links or files shared through social media can lead to malware infections.

Account hijacking: Weak security practices can make it easy for attackers to gain unauthorized access to social media accounts.

Key Strategies for Social Media Security

Privacy Settings: Regularly review and adjust your privacy settings to control who can see your posts, contact you, and find your profile on social media platforms. Opt for the most restrictive settings that still allow you to use the platform as desired.

Strong Passwords: Use strong, unique passwords for each social media account. Consider using a password manager to generate and store complex passwords securely.

Two-Factor Authentication (2FA): Enable 2FA on all social media accounts to add an extra layer of security, making it harder for unauthorized users to gain access even if they have your password.

Be Skeptical of Links and Attachments: Exercise caution when clicking on links or downloading attachments from social media, even if they appear to come from friends. Verify the authenticity of messages that seem unusual or out of character.

Limit Personal Information Sharing: Be mindful of the amount and type of personal information you share on social media. Avoid posting details that could be used to steal your identity, such as your full date of birth, address, or confidential family information.

Review Connected Apps: Periodically review and remove apps or services connected to your social media accounts that are no longer needed or appear suspicious.

Educate Yourself and Others: Stay informed about the latest social media scams and threats. Educate friends and family, especially those who may be less familiar with these risks.

Regularly Monitor Accounts: Keep an eye on your social media accounts for any unusual activity, such as posts you did not make, unexpected messages sent from your account, or unauthorized changes to your profile information.

Dealing with Compromised Accounts

If you suspect your social media account has been compromised:

Change Your Password Immediately: If possible, log in and change your password to something strong and unique.

Check Account Settings: Review your account settings for any changes made by the attacker, such as altered email addresses or added connected apps.

Notify Your Contacts: Inform your contacts not to engage with any suspicious messages sent from your account during the period it was compromised.

Report to the Platform: Use the platform's reporting tools to notify them of the compromise so they can take appropriate action.

As social media continues to play a significant role in daily life, adopting robust security practices is crucial for protecting oneself against the myriad of threats present on these platforms. By implementing the strategies outlined in this chapter, users can enjoy the benefits of social media while minimizing their vulnerability to cyber threats. Remember, security is not just about protecting data; it's about safeguarding your digital identity and presence in the vast social media landscape.

PROTECTING YOUR ONLINE IDENTITY AND PERSONAL DATA

In the digital age, our online identity and personal data are as valuable as physical assets, making the protection of these digital assets paramount. Cybercriminals continuously devise new methods to exploit personal information for fraudulent activities, identity theft, and financial gain. This chapter outlines strategies for safeguarding your online identity and personal data against such threats.

Understanding the Value of Personal Data

Personal data encompasses a wide range of information, including names, addresses, email addresses, passwords, financial details, and social security numbers. This information can be used by cybercriminals to commit fraud, access bank accounts, open new accounts in your name, or even for extortion purposes. Recognizing the value of this data is the first step in protecting it.

Strategies for Protecting Personal Data

Guard Your Information: Be cautious about the information you share online, especially on social media. Adjust privacy settings to limit who can see your posts and personal information.

Use Strong, Unique Passwords: Employ complex passwords and use a different password for each online account. Consider using a reputable password manager to keep track of your passwords securely.

Enable Two-Factor Authentication (2FA): Wherever possible, activate 2FA on your online accounts. This adds an additional layer of security, making it more difficult for attackers to gain unauthorized access.

Be Wary of Phishing Attempts: Educate yourself on recognizing phishing emails or messages that attempt to trick you into providing personal information. Verify the authenticity of requests by contacting the company directly through official channels.

Secure Your Devices: Keep your devices secure with up-to-date antivirus software, firewalls, and regular software updates. These measures can help protect your devices from malware that could capture your personal information.

Monitor Financial Transactions: Regularly check your bank statements and credit reports for any unauthorized transactions or accounts opened in your name. Early detection of fraudulent activity can mitigate potential damage.

Use Secure Connections: Avoid transmitting sensitive information over public Wi-Fi networks. Use a virtual private network (VPN) to encrypt your internet connection when using public or untrusted networks.

Educate Family Members: Ensure that all family members, especially children and elderly relatives, are aware of the importance of online privacy and the risks associated with sharing personal information online.

Know Your Rights: Familiarize yourself with the privacy policies of websites and online services you use. Understand how your data is collected, used, and protected under laws and regulations like the GDPR or CCPA.

Dealing with Data Breaches

If you learn that your personal data may have been compromised in a data breach:

Change Passwords Immediately: Update passwords for the affected accounts and any other accounts using the same passwords.

Monitor for Fraud: Keep an eye on bank accounts and credit reports for signs of unauthorized activity.

Alert Affected Institutions: Notify your bank, credit card issuers, and other relevant institutions about the potential breach of your personal data.

Consider a Credit Freeze: To prevent new accounts from being opened in your name, consider placing a freeze on your credit with the major credit bureaus.

Protecting your online identity and personal data requires vigilance, proactive measures, and an ongoing commitment to security practices. By implementing the strategies outlined in this chapter, individuals can significantly reduce their vulnerability to identity theft and other forms of cybercrime, ensuring their digital well-being in an increasingly connected world.

UNDERSTANDING THE THREAT LANDSCAPE FOR BUSINESSES

In an increasingly digital world, businesses of all sizes face a complex array of cybersecurity threats. From sophisticated cyber-attacks targeting corporate data to insider threats that compromise internal security, understanding the threat landscape is essential for developing effective defense strategies. This chapter provides an overview of the current cybersecurity threats facing businesses and offers insights into preparing and protecting against these evolving challenges.

Cybersecurity Threats to Businesses

Ransomware Attacks: One of the most disruptive types of cyber-attacks, ransomware encrypts a company's data, rendering it inaccessible until a ransom is paid. The impact can range from operational disruption to significant financial losses and data breaches.

Phishing Scams: Phishing remains a prevalent threat, with attackers using deceptive emails to trick employees into revealing sensitive information or downloading malware. Spear-phishing targets specific individuals within an organization, often using personalized information to increase the likelihood of success.

Data Breaches: Unauthorized access to company data can lead to the theft of intellectual property, customer information, and other sensitive data. Data breaches can result from external attacks or insider threats and can have severe reputational and financial consequences.

Insider Threats: Not all threats come from outside the organization. Disgruntled employees, negligence, or inadequate access controls can lead to insider threats, where individuals misuse their access to company resources for personal gain or to inflict damage.

Advanced Persistent Threats (APTs): APTs are sophisticated, long-term cyber-attacks where attackers gain access to a network and remain undetected for extended periods. The goal is often to steal data systematically or to monitor and disrupt business activities.

Supply Chain Attacks: Attackers increasingly target less-secure elements in a company's supply chain to gain access to the larger organization's network. These attacks can compromise software vendors, hardware suppliers, or service providers.

DDoS Attacks: Distributed Denial of Service (DDoS) attacks flood a company's web services with excessive traffic, overwhelming systems and making them unavailable to legitimate users. This can lead to operational disruptions and damage customer trust.

Preparing and Protecting Against Cyber Threats

Cybersecurity Awareness Training: Educate employees about

the importance of cybersecurity, how to recognize phishing attempts, and the proper handling of company data. Regular training can significantly reduce the risk of successful attacks.

Implement Robust Security Measures: Utilize firewalls, antivirus software, encryption, and intrusion detection systems to protect against external threats. Regularly update and patch systems to fix vulnerabilities.

Access Controls and Monitoring: Limit access to sensitive data to only those employees who need it to perform their job functions. Implement monitoring tools to detect unusual access patterns or data movement within the network.

Incident Response Plan: Develop and regularly update an incident response plan that outlines steps to take in the event of a cybersecurity incident. This plan should include communication strategies, roles and responsibilities, and recovery processes.

Regular Security Assessments: Conduct regular security assessments and penetration testing to identify vulnerabilities within the network. This proactive approach allows businesses to address weaknesses before they can be exploited.

Backup and Recovery Processes: Maintain regular backups of critical data and establish clear recovery processes. In the event of data loss due to ransomware or other cyber-attacks, having up-to-date backups can be crucial for restoring operations.

The cybersecurity threat landscape for businesses is dynamic and requires constant vigilance and adaptation. By understanding the types of threats and implementing comprehensive security measures, businesses can mitigate risks and protect their assets, employees, and customers from potential harm. Collaboration, education, and investment in cybersecurity infrastructure are key to navigating the challenges of the digital age.

INTRODUCTION TO COMPLIANCE AND STANDARDS

In the realm of cybersecurity and data protection, compliance with regulatory standards is not just a legal requirement but also a cornerstone of trust and safety for individuals and businesses alike. Regulations like the General Data Protection Regulation (GDPR) in the European Union and the Health Insurance Portability and Accountability Act (HIPAA) in the United States set the benchmarks for privacy, security, and compliance in handling personal and sensitive information. This chapter provides an overview of these and other critical standards, elucidating their importance and impact on business practices.

The General Data Protection Regulation (GDPR)

Implemented in May 2018, the GDPR represents a landmark in the protection of personal data for individuals within the European Union and the European Economic Area. It also addresses the transfer of personal data outside the EU and EEA areas. The GDPR's core principles revolve around the lawful, fair, and transparent processing of personal data, with a strong emphasis on the rights of individuals. These rights include the right to access, correct, delete, and restrict the processing of personal data, as well as the right to data portability.

Businesses and organizations that process the personal data of EU citizens, regardless of the company's location, must comply with the GDPR. Non-compliance can result in significant fines, up to €20 million or 4% of the company's global annual revenue, whichever is higher.

The Health Insurance Portability and Accountability Act (HIPAA)

HIPAA, enacted in 1996 in the United States, establishes national standards to protect sensitive patient health information from being disclosed without the patient's consent or knowledge. The Act applies to health care providers, health plans, and health care clearinghouses, as well as to business associates that process health information on their behalf.

HIPAA compliance involves ensuring the confidentiality, integrity, and availability of protected health information (PHI), implementing safeguards to protect the information, and ensuring compliance by their workforce. Violations of HIPAA can lead to substantial financial penalties and reputational damage.

Other Notable Standards and Regulations

PCI DSS (Payment Card Industry Data Security Standard): A global standard that mandates security measures for organizations that handle credit and debit card information to protect against fraud and data breaches.

SOX (Sarbanes-Oxley Act): A United States federal law that mandates certain practices in financial record keeping and reporting for corporations to protect investors from fraudulent activities.

ISO/IEC 27001: Part of the ISO/IEC 27000 family of standards, ISO/IEC 27001 is an information security standard that specifies a management system aimed at bringing information security under explicit management control.

Implementing Compliance and Security Standards

Adhering to compliance and security standards requires a comprehensive understanding of the regulations, a commitment to implementing necessary policies and procedures, and ongoing monitoring and improvement of security practices. Steps include:

Conducting Risk Assessments: Identifying potential risks to personal or sensitive data and evaluating the effectiveness of current controls.

Developing Policies and Procedures: Establishing clear policies and procedures that comply with legal requirements and best practices for data protection.

Training and Awareness: Educating employees about compliance requirements and best practices for data protection.

Implementing Technical Safeguards: Using encryption, access controls, and other security measures to protect data.

Regular Audits and Reviews: Continuously monitoring and reviewing compliance status and making adjustments as necessary.

Compliance with data protection and security standards is essential for protecting sensitive information and maintaining trust in the digital age. By understanding and implementing the principles of GDPR, HIPAA, and other relevant standards, organizations can not only avoid legal penalties but also strengthen their reputation and competitive advantage in the marketplace.

MALWARE IN DEPTH

Malware, short for malicious software, presents a significant threat to computer security. It infiltrates computer systems to execute harmful actions, such as pilfering sensitive data, corrupting files, or causing disruptions. Grasping the diverse forms of malware and their operational mechanisms is crucial. Each malware instance comprises two key elements: a propagation mechanism and a payload. The propagation mechanism enables the malware to spread from one system to another, with the methods varying among different types of malware. Shortly, we'll explore three distinct malware types and their dissemination methods. The payload, on the other hand, is the damaging action executed by the malware. For instance, malware could sift through your hard drive for financial documents or encrypt files until a ransom is paid, or it might log keystrokes to capture banking credentials. We'll delve deeper into various payloads in an upcoming segment.

The initial malware type to consider is the computer virus. While most are familiar with viruses, the term is often mistakenly applied to all malware forms. Analogous to biological viruses, the defining feature of a computer virus is its reliance on user actions for transmission. This could involve opening a malicious email attachment, visiting a harmful website, or using an infected USB drive. Viruses cannot proliferate without human assistance, making user education a vital defense strategy.

The second malware category is the worm. Unlike viruses, worms propagate autonomously, without needing human interaction. They exploit system vulnerabilities to spread, using each infected system as a launchpad to further infiltrate networks. The most effective defense against worms is to regularly update systems with the latest software patches, eliminating vulnerabilities they might exploit.

Historically significant, worms date back to 1988 with the RTM Worm, initiated by Robert Tappan Morris. This early worm incident, infecting about 10% of the then-smaller internet, underscored the importance of internet security, a concern previously underestimated by network administrators.

In 2010, the Stuxnet worm targeted a uranium enrichment facility in Iran, marking a notable incident where a worm caused physical damage. By infecting systems controlling uranium centrifuges, Stuxnet forced them to malfunction, significantly impacting Iran's nuclear program.

The final malware type we address is the Trojan Horse, named after the ancient Greek stratagem. Trojans disguise themselves as legitimate software, enticing users to download and install them. While performing as expected, they also unleash harmful actions unbeknownst to the user. Since Trojans gain entry through software installations, application control is an effective countermeasure, restricting software execution to administrator-approved applications.

Remote Access Trojans (RATs), a subset of Trojans, provide attackers remote control over infected systems, underscoring the diverse threats posed by malware.

Understanding the distinctions among viruses, worms, and Trojan Horses is essential, highlighting the need for vigilant cybersecurity measures tailored to combat each malware type's unique dissemination methods.

Malware, the shorthand for malicious software, stands as a formidable adversary in computer security, sneaking into systems to unleash harmful actions such as data theft, file damage, or system disruption. A deep understanding of malware's anatomy is pivotal. Each malware instance consists of a method for spreading, known as a propagation mechanism, and a payload that executes the malicious intent. Previously, we've discussed how malware spreads. Now, we'll examine four distinct malware payloads: adware, spyware, ransomware, and cryptomalware, starting with adware.

Adware: The Covert Advertiser

Online advertising mirrors its counterparts in traditional media as a prevalent revenue source. Usually, it's a legitimate exchange: content providers earn revenue, and advertisers gain exposure. However, where there's profit, malware often lurks. Adware hijacks this model, displaying unsolicited ads to users, funneling revenue not to the content creators but to the malware developers. Methods vary, from redirecting search queries to displaying intrusive pop-ups, potentially masquerading as legitimate site content. The impact of adware ranges from a mere nuisance to a significant threat, particularly from the content creator's perspective.

Spyware: The Silent Snooper

Spyware operates covertly, collecting information without consent. The gathered data, ranging from personal identifiers to financial details, is a goldmine for malicious actors aiming for identity theft or espionage. Spyware can deploy keyloggers to capture keystrokes, monitor web activity, or even search directly on a user's system for valuable information. Often, spyware sneaks onto systems bundled with desired software, slipping past users during installation. These programs, sometimes categorized as potentially unwanted programs (PUPs), can pose serious privacy and security risks.

Ransomware: The Digital Kidnapper

Ransomware takes control of a computer or encrypts files, demanding payment for restoration. A notorious example, WannaCry, exploited the EternalBlue vulnerability in 2017, encrypting user files and demanding Bitcoin ransoms. The dilemma with ransomware is whether to pay the ransom. While funding criminals is objectionable, the desperation to recover encrypted files leads over 40% of victims to pay up, with ransomware like CryptoLocker amassing over $27 million.

Cryptomalware: The Crypto Miner

Cryptomalware commandeers computing resources to mine cryptocurrencies, benefiting the malware author. It's crucial not to conflate cryptomalware with ransomware; the former focuses on cryptocurrency mining using the victim's computing power, while the latter encrypts files for ransom. The key to their names lies in the attacker's goal: ransomware seeks a ransom, whereas cryptomalware aims to generate cryptocurrency.

Defending Against Malware

Protection against malware involves a multifaceted strategy:

Antivirus Software: Install and regularly update antivirus software to catch and neutralize malware threats.

Security Patches: Apply system and application patches promptly to close vulnerabilities that could be exploited by malware.

User Education: Inform users about malware risks and safe computing practices to prevent inadvertent malware introductions.

Malware payloads, diverse in their objectives, collectively pose a significant risk to system security and user privacy. Aspiring security professionals must equip themselves to guard organizations against the full spectrum of malware threats, ensuring the integrity and confidentiality of systems and data in an ever-evolving cybersecurity landscape.

EMBEDDED THREATS: BACKDOORS AND LOGIC BOMBS

In our exploration of malware, we've encountered various types such as viruses, worms, Trojan horses, adware, spyware, and ransomware. These threats typically manifest as standalone programs created by malicious actors to execute harmful activities. However, not all malware operates independently. Some are intricately woven into legitimate applications, serving nefarious purposes from within. This section delves into two such insidious forms of malware: backdoors and logic bombs.

The Hidden Passages: Backdoors

Backdoors are secret pathways into systems, intentionally created by developers for seemingly benign reasons, such as simplifying maintenance tasks or providing emergency access to locked-out users. Despite these good intentions, backdoors can inadvertently compromise security. Customers might not appreciate undisclosed access routes into their systems, and these backdoors could become known to malicious entities, especially if documented publicly, such as in user manuals.

Backdoors can manifest through various means, including hardcoded credentials, which are preset usernames and passwords, default passwords that users may overlook changing, or undisclosed access methods bypassing standard authentication. A notable portrayal of a backdoor was in the 1983 film "War Games," where the protagonist gains administrative access to a military computer using the system creator's son's name, "Joshua."

Real-world instances include the discovery of a backdoor in Samsung Galaxy devices in 2014, allowing remote data access, and in 2015, reports emerged about credit card readers compromised through default passwords. Surprisingly, I even found a default username and password in my sprinkler system's manual, a potential oversight by many users.

The Ticking Time Bombs: Logic Bombs

Logic bombs are malware coded to activate under specific conditions, such as a particular date and time, alterations in file content, or certain API call outcomes. These hidden threats lie dormant until their activation criteria are met, unleashing their payload without warning. A hypothetical scenario involves a disgruntled programmer embedding a logic bomb in a payroll system to check for their employment status; if removed from the payroll, the bomb detonates, executing a retaliatory action.

Historically, logic bombs have caused notable disruptions, including a 2003 incident impacting South Korean government systems. Another infamous case is the "Friday the 13th" logic bomb, which remained inactive until meeting its specific date-triggered condition, demonstrating the longstanding threat of logic bombs.

Safeguarding Against Embedded Malware

To defend against the hidden dangers of backdoors and logic bombs, security professionals must employ vigilance alongside traditional anti-malware measures. Regularly updating default passwords, deactivating unnecessary accounts, and staying informed through security bulletins about potential vulnerabilities in software are crucial practices. These steps help mitigate the risks posed by these embedded threats, ensuring the integrity and security of organizational systems and data.

Malware creators are adept, highly skilled software engineers who are well-versed in the detection and prevention strategies employed by cybersecurity professionals. This knowledge drives them to devise complex methods to evade detection and circumvent conventional anti-malware measures. Let's delve into two sophisticated types of malware: rootkits and fileless viruses.

The root account holds supreme privileges on systems, granting complete control over system resources. Typically, this level of access is intended solely for system administrators. However, gaining root access is a common objective among hackers. Rootkits began as tools for escalating privileges; an attacker would first compromise a standard user account, then deploy a rootkit to elevate this access to superuser status. Over time, the definition of rootkits has expanded to include software that conceals the presence of certain programs on a system. Rootkits can serve various purposes, ranging from creating backdoors and forming botnets to distributing adware or spyware. Interestingly, not all rootkits are designed with harmful intent; some aim to protect copyrighted content as an anti-theft measure.

The security of computer systems is often conceptualized through a ring protection model, which categorizes program access levels to system resources. While most applications operate under restricted user mode privileges, the operating system functions in a highly privileged kernel mode. Rootkits can operate in both user mode, where they are simpler to create but harder to detect, and kernel mode, which grants them extensive privileges but makes them easier to identify and challenging to develop.

Fileless viruses represent another strategy for eluding straightforward antivirus detection by avoiding disk storage entirely and operating solely in a computer's memory. Various techniques enable fileless viruses to infect systems and persist without leaving any files behind. An early instance of a fileless virus could be seen in Microsoft Office macro viruses, which utilized the Office scripting language. Contemporary fileless viruses might execute as JavaScript downloaded from a website or achieve persistence by embedding themselves in the Windows registry. This method allows them to be reloaded into memory upon system reboot, maintaining their presence without traditional file storage.

BOTNETS IN DEPTH

We've explored various methods through which cybercriminals can hijack a single computer using malware, with certain types, like worms, having the capability to autonomously propagate and infect additional systems. A prevalent motive for cybercriminals commandeering computers is to exploit their processing power, storage capacity, or internet bandwidth by incorporating them into botnets. Botnets are networks of compromised computers, often referred to as zombie computers, harnessed for nefarious activities. The process of forming a botnet starts with the initial infection of a computer using malware distributed via any previously mentioned techniques. Once a cybercriminal gains control over a computer, it is assimilated into the botnet and remains inactive until activated by the botnet's controller.

What purposes do botnets serve? Typically, the creators of botnets don't directly utilize them. Instead, they lease or sell access to the botnet to third parties interested in sending bulk spam, launching distributed denial-of-service (DDoS) attacks, mining for cryptocurrencies, or conducting password cracking operations. Essentially, any activity that benefits from hijacked computing resources can be a potential use case for a botnet.

Managing a botnet requires discrete communication channels to relay commands from the cybercriminal to the compromised machines without detection. Direct communication is avoidable as it would lead to swift interception by security teams. Cybercriminals employ various indirect command-and-control (C&C) methods to obscure their operations and location. These include utilizing internet relay chat (IRC) channels, social media accounts, or establishing peer-to-peer communications within the botnet. Given the constant threat of disruption by security efforts, these C&C mechanisms are designed to be highly resilient, ensuring the longevity of the botnet's control.

Summarizing the lifecycle of a botnet: it begins with the malware infection of numerous global systems, which are then transformed into botnet nodes. These compromised units might further disseminate the malware, expanding the botnet. Subsequently, they connect to a C&C network constructed by the botnet operator to fetch directives, which are typically executed in the form of spam distribution or DDoS assaults.

For cybersecurity experts, comprehending how devices are conscripted into botnets, the operational use of botnets by cybercriminals, and the intricacies of C&C mechanisms is critical. Equipped with this understanding, you can better identify and counteract botnet activities within your network.

MALICIOUS SCRIPT EXECUTION

During our discussion on fileless viruses, we touched upon instances where cyber attackers might attempt to run harmful scripts on a user's system. Let's delve further into this concept of executing malicious scripts. Essentially, scripts are sequences of commands directed at a computer, instructing it to perform specified actions. We frequently utilize scripts to automate repetitive tasks or simplify complex operations. Scripts are omnipresent, embedded in operating systems, hosted on web platforms, and incorporated within various applications. Computers execute scripts in several contexts. Shell scripts, executed via command line, are closely tied to operating system functions, enabling script authors to manipulate files and conduct system-level operations. Application-specific scripts interact with and automate actions within particular software, while general-purpose programming languages offer the flexibility to script a wide array of activities.

Understanding the role and mechanics of scripting is crucial. However, it's equally important to recognize the potential for scripts to be weaponized. Malicious scripts crafted by attackers can facilitate unauthorized access, alter file permissions, among other malicious activities. Hence, caution is paramount when deciding which scripts to run on systems you manage.

Acquainting yourself with several key scripting languages is advisable. Here's a brief overview:

Bash: Predominantly used on Linux and macOS, Bash is a shell scripting language revered by system administrators for its seamless integration with these operating systems.

PowerShell: For Windows environments, PowerShell is the equivalent, empowering administrators to automate a myriad of Windows-specific tasks.

Macros and VBA (Visual Basic for Applications): Within application ecosystems, particularly the Microsoft Office Suite, VBA is a predominant macro scripting language, enabling task automation within these applications.

Python: As a versatile, general-purpose scripting language, Python is favored among developers for its capability to tackle nearly any programming challenge, contributing to its widespread popularity.

While learning cybersecurity, familiarizing yourself with PowerShell, Bash, VBA, macros, and Python is beneficial. Proficiency in coding in these languages isn't required, but an understanding of their typical applications is.

UNDERSTANDING ATTACKERS

Cybersecurity professionals are tasked with safeguarding their organizations from a myriad of threats. Throughout your career in cybersecurity, you're likely to encounter attackers of varying sophistication, resources, and motivations. Let's explore these differences. Attacks can originate from both within and outside an organization. While the immediate thought often goes to external threats, internal sources can present a significant risk due to their authorized access to the organization's systems. We'll delve deeper into the insider threat shortly.

Attackers vary greatly in their technical skills, access to resources, their driving motives, and ultimate objectives. On one end of the spectrum, we have the novice individual hacker, driven by curiosity to breach systems, and on the other, highly organized state-sponsored groups wielding vast resources.

Script Kiddies: Positioned at the lower end of the technical skill spectrum, these individuals rely on pre-written scripts to conduct attacks, lacking the expertise to develop their own hacking tools. Basic security measures like timely software updates and standard security solutions are usually sufficient to thwart their efforts.

Hacktivists: These attackers can range from minimally skilled to highly proficient in technical skills, united by their use of hacking to further political or social causes. The term hacktivist blends 'hacker' with 'activist', indicating their mission-driven motives.

Organized Crime: Increasingly, cybercrime has seen the involvement of criminal groups, orchestrating ransomware and cyber extortion schemes for financial gain. These groups often possess sophisticated technical abilities.

Corporate Espionage: Here, the motive is to gain a competitive edge by unlawly acquiring proprietary information from rivals. An illustrative case is the 2017 incident involving the St. Louis Cardinals and the Houston Astros, where a hacking attack aimed to steal vital player information.

Nation-State Actors: Representing the pinnacle of cyber threats, nation-state or state-sponsored actors conduct highly sophisticated cyber operations. Known as Advanced Persistent Threat (APT) groups, these attackers, possibly military units or similarly trained, utilize cutting-edge techniques and are notoriously hard to detect. While often assumed to target government entities exclusively, they also pursue civilian objectives that align with national interests.

In the hacker lexicon, inspired by classic Western films, we categorize hackers by "hat" colors:

White Hat Hackers: Operate with authorization, aiming to uncover and remedy security vulnerabilities.

Black Hat Hackers: Engage in unauthorized, malicious hacking.

Gray Hat Hackers: Operate without permission, not necessarily with malicious intent, aiming to identify and perhaps even fix security issues, though their actions are illegal and ethically questionable.

It's vital to grasp the nuances of these attacker profiles.

Understanding an adversary's motives is a key element in crafting effective defenses against their strategies.

INSIDER THREATS

While external threats are often highlighted, some of the most significant and damaging attacks come from within an organization itself. Insider threats, posed by current or former employees, contractors, and other individuals with inside access, can be particularly perilous. These insiders might misuse their access to pilfer data or funds, or to inflict harm upon the organization. The data on insider threats is stark: over half of organizations that suffered a security breach were compromised by an insider, and in two-thirds of these incidents, the breaches carried out by insiders with privileged access proved costlier to rectify than those conducted externally. Often, these breaches are executed by highly trusted individuals, such as system administrators or high-level executives, although not exclusively through high-level accounts. Attacks might involve elevating a regular user's access to that of a superuser, leveraging undisclosed technical skills or assistance from knowledgeable acquaintances.

To mitigate insider threats, organizations can adopt several human resource strategies:

Background Checks: Screening potential employees can reveal any previous legal entanglements or behaviors that could signal risk.

Least Privilege Principle: Ensuring individuals have only the access necessary for their job functions can limit potential damage.

Two-Person Control: For sensitive actions, such as financial transactions, requiring dual approval can add an extra layer of security.

Mandatory Vacations: Enforcing vacation policies for critical roles can expose ongoing fraudulent schemes, as the absence of the perpetrator breaks the continuity of their cover-up.

Vigilance for signs of misuse and designing security protocols that minimize potential insider damage is crucial for organizational safety. Another aspect of insider-related risk is "Shadow IT," where employees introduce unauthorized technology into the workplace. These unsanctioned tools can significantly elevate security risks by bypassing established security measures. Monitoring for and addressing the use of Shadow IT is essential in safeguarding an organization's cybersecurity posture.

ATTACK VECTORS

Before a cyber attacker can compromise our systems or infiltrate our networks, they must first identify a point of entry. These entry points, known as attack vectors, are the methods attackers exploit to gain initial access. Let's examine some prevalent attack vectors within the current cybersecurity landscape.

Email: This is a widely utilized attack vector. Cybercriminals dispatch emails with phishing attempts or embed malicious attachments and links, aiming to deceive an employee into inadvertently providing access to the organization's network. Ransomware, for instance, can spread through just one misplaced click by an unsuspecting user, risking the security of the entire organization.

Social Media: Besides being a platform for spreading malware similarly to email, social media can also play a role in manipulation campaigns. These efforts aim to build trust with users who might then be manipulated into providing access to sensitive information and systems. This blend of digital attacks with psychological tactics seeks to alter the behavior of employees, customers, and other key individuals.

Removable Media: Devices like USB drives represent another vector for malware dissemination. Cybercriminals might leave USB drives in public spots, betting on curious finders to connect them to their computers. This action can trigger a stealthy malware attack, giving attackers a foothold in the user's system. Similarly, seemingly innocuous USB cables with embedded malicious chips can serve the same purpose.

Magnetic Stripe Cards: Vulnerable to skimming attacks, magnetic stripe cards can be compromised through devices attached to ATMs, gas pumps, and similar terminals. These skimmers capture card data, enabling attackers to clone the card for fraudulent transactions.

Cloud Services: Attackers often probe cloud services for misconfigured files, security vulnerabilities, or exposed sensitive data like API keys or passwords. It's crucial for organizations to incorporate cloud security into their overall security strategy.

Physical Access: Direct physical access to systems or networks opens another avenue for attacks. Unprotected network ports in public areas or physical access to computers and network devices can lead to unauthorized control. This risk extends beyond the organization's premises, with potential interference in the IT supply chain allowing attackers to tamper with devices before they reach the end user.

Wireless Networks: An insecure wireless network provides an attacker with a straightforward route into an organization's network from a distance, such as from a parking lot. Weakly secured wireless networks are a considerable security liability.

Recognizing these varied attack vectors is crucial for cybersecurity professionals. By understanding the tactics employed by cyber adversaries, we can enhance our defenses and protect our systems and networks more effectively.

One of the primary avenues through which organizations become susceptible to cyber attacks is the failure to promptly apply security patches. This oversight leaves systems vulnerable to attackers equipped with the knowledge to exploit these gaps. The remedy seems straightforward: apply security updates from vendors as soon as they become available to bolster defenses. However, the challenge is that not every vulnerability is known. Modern operating systems, with their millions of lines of code, inevitably harbor undiscovered security flaws that pose latent risks.

When security experts uncover new vulnerabilities, they typically proceed in a responsible manner, informing the affected vendor to allow for remediation before making the issue public. This process effectively addresses countless vulnerabilities each year. But the scenario shifts when an individual discovers a vulnerability and chooses secrecy over disclosure, converting this knowledge into a covert tool for unauthorized access. Such undisclosed vulnerabilities are termed zero-day vulnerabilities, possessing immense power until they are eventually uncovered by the wider community. The absence of a patch for these vulnerabilities renders standard security measures, like patches and intrusion detection systems, ineffective during the window of vulnerability—the period between the vulnerability's discovery and the availability of a patch.

Exploiting a zero-day requires specific knowledge, tools, and skills, making it an unlikely weapon in the arsenal of average attackers. However, Advanced Persistent Threats (APTs) — sophisticated, well-funded attackers such as military units, intelligence agencies, or organized groups focusing on high-value targets — are known to employ zero-days among other advanced techniques. These adversaries are termed "advanced" due to their technical capabilities, including access to zero-days, and "persistent" for their relentless pursuit of specific, valuable targets.

Defending against APTs poses significant challenges due to their skillful use of zero-day vulnerabilities, allowing them to breach the defenses of most organizations. Competing against the resources of a well-funded entity is daunting for any organization, large or small. Nonetheless, adopting robust security practices, such as employing strong encryption and conducting thorough monitoring, can provide a degree of protection, helping safeguard sensitive information against APT attacks.

THREAT INTELLIGENCE

Threat intelligence forms an indispensable pillar of any organization's cybersecurity framework, enabling entities to stay abreast of evolving cyber threats. At its core, threat intelligence encompasses the efforts undertaken by organizations to keep informed about the shifting cybersecurity landscape and to incorporate knowledge of emerging threats into their cybersecurity protocols.

The internet is awash with data on cybersecurity threats, to the extent that one could dedicate their entire working hours to staying updated on cybersecurity developments. However, not everyone has the luxury of time to engage in such extensive reading, though it remains essential for security professionals to keep pace with the latest trends in the field. The process of sourcing this information from publicly accessible resources is termed open-source intelligence. Prominent sources of open-source intelligence include security-focused websites, databases cataloging vulnerabilities, mainstream and social media, disclosures found on the dark web, both public and private threat-sharing platforms, as well as repositories hosting files and code, and organizations dedicated to security research.

Certain methods for gathering intelligence are straightforward and can be employed by both threat actors and security teams. For instance, adversaries might engage in email harvesting to compile lists of potential targets for phishing campaigns by scouring the internet for valid email addresses associated with a particular domain.

Sifting through the vast expanse of open-source intelligence can be an arduous task, and many organizations lack the resources to delve deeply into this sea of data to extract actionable insights. This gap has given rise to a specialized threat intelligence industry, offering products and services that deliver proprietary threat intelligence, leveraging predictive analytics. These offerings range from succinct briefings on critical security developments to IP reputation services providing up-to-the-minute data on IP addresses known for malicious activities. Such intelligence feeds can be integrated directly into firewalls, intrusion detection systems, and other security mechanisms, enabling organizations to preemptively block access from suspicious IP addresses.

While real-time threat maps published by some security firms may appear more as eye-catching marketing tools than practical security solutions, they offer a captivating view of the cyber threats being tracked.

With a plethora of information sources at your disposal, evaluating their fit within your security strategy is crucial. Consider three key factors when assessing a threat intelligence source:

Timeliness: How swiftly does the source update its information following the emergence or evolution of a new threat?

Accuracy: Does the source reliably report correct information?

Reliability: Does the source consistently provide timely and accurate intelligence in a manner that aligns with your organizational needs?

By judiciously selecting and utilizing threat intelligence sources based on these criteria, organizations can enhance their cybersecurity posture and better navigate the complex landscape of cyber threats.

THREAT INDICATORS

Managing threat information effectively is crucial for cybersecurity operations, and at the heart of this process are threat indicators. These indicators include specific details such as IP addresses, signatures of malicious files, communication patterns, and other unique identifiers that help pinpoint potential cyber threats. For threat intelligence to be impactful, it must be shareable among stakeholders. The challenge arises in how to share this information, especially in an automated and standardized manner, to ensure seamless communication across diverse systems and organizations.

The cornerstone of successful threat information sharing lies in adopting a common language or framework. This is where several key frameworks come into play, facilitating the categorization, communication, and exchange of cybersecurity information.

Cyber Observable eXpression (CybOX): This framework offers a standardized schema for detailing cybersecurity observations, allowing analysts to classify various security events effectively. By defining the attributes of cybersecurity incidents, CybOX aids in the consistent description of threats.

Structured Threat Information eXpression (STIX): Building upon CybOX's foundational schema, STIX provides a language for articulating detailed security information in a structured format. This standardized language enhances the clarity and precision of threat communication between different systems and organizations.

Trusted Automated eXchange of Indicator Information (TAXII): TAXII complements STIX by providing the technical means for the actual exchange of security information. Through a set of protocols and services, TAXII facilitates the automated sharing of STIX-formatted threat data among entities.

These frameworks, developed through community-driven efforts and supported by the US Department of Homeland Security, represent a cohesive approach to threat intelligence management. The DHS website visually delineates how STIX, TAXII, and CybOX interconnect, with CybOX serving as the schema for threat classification, STIX for defining information elements, and TAXII for enabling the exchange of this information.

While the focus is on STIX and TAXII, understanding CybOX's role provides a comprehensive view of how these elements synergize. Additionally, OpenIOC, another framework devised by FireEye's Mandiant team, offers an alternative method for describing and disseminating threat information. OpenIOC, for instance, might describe a malicious file named "evil.exe" implicated in financial cybercrimes, detailing specific characteristics such as associated services or file sizes that signal a security threat.

To maximize the utility of threat intelligence, it's pivotal that security tools within an organization are configured to both generate and interpret threat indicators in these standardized formats. Automating the sharing and reception of threat data not only streamlines the workload of security analysts but also enhances the overall efficacy of cybersecurity measures.

Threat Intelligence Sharing

Recently, we delved into the technological foundations supporting the exchange of threat intelligence across an organization's systems, spotlighting frameworks like TAXII, STIX, and CybOX. These tools are particularly effective when leveraged to disseminate threat data among colleagues, across different departments within an enterprise, and even among distinct organizations. Reflect on the diverse business units within your organization that would gain insights from access to threat intelligence. Several key areas could substantially benefit from shared threat intelligence, including:

Incident Response Teams: Dedicated to promptly addressing security incidents.

Vulnerability Management Teams: Focused on identifying and mitigating potential security vulnerabilities.

Risk Management Teams: Charged with the comprehensive assessment of cybersecurity risks.

Security Engineering Teams: Tasked with crafting safeguards against evolving cyber threats.

Detection and Monitoring Teams: Responsible for continuous surveillance of the security landscape for potential threats, such as those within a Security Operations Center.

The integration of technology frameworks for threat intelligence facilitates the seamless exchange of critical data amongst the various specialized functions, enriching the collective cybersecurity posture. The value of shared intelligence is magnified when extended across different organizations, fostering a collaborative defense ecosystem.

To support this collaborative effort, Information Sharing and Analysis Centers (ISACs) play a pivotal role. ISACs convene cybersecurity professionals from across industry lines, including direct competitors, to share sector-specific security insights confidentially. The primary aim of ISACs is to circulate threat intelligence without compromising participants' anonymity, creating a secure platform for mutual cooperation among industry peers.

A glance at the roster of existing ISACs reveals a broad spectrum covering various sectors, from automotive and aviation to communications, defense, and even specialized fields like natural gas and election security. Virtually every industry is represented by one or more ISACs, typically operating as non-profit entities, making participation both impactful and cost-efficient.

For those involved in cybersecurity, identifying and joining the ISAC relevant to your industry is a strategic move. Participating in these information-sharing initiatives not only bolsters your organization's defenses but also contributes to the broader community's resilience against cyber threats.

Threat intelligence plays a pivotal role in enhancing our comprehension of the cybersecurity landscape. By dissecting the motives and capabilities of cyber adversaries, organizations can refine their defense strategies against potential attacks. The essence of threat research lies in delving deep into the psyche of these adversaries, employing threat intelligence as a lens to anticipate and mitigate their next moves.

There are two fundamental approaches to conducting effective threat research:

Reputational Threat Research: This method involves identifying and tracking entities known for previous malicious activities. By leveraging historical data from defense systems, such as records of malevolent IP addresses, email addresses, or domains, organizations can preemptively block these known threats from accessing their systems again. This process of attributing a reputation score to each entity helps in safeguarding the organization from entities with a history of malicious intent.

Behavioral Threat Research: This technique focuses on detecting anomalous behavior that mirrors the tactics employed by attackers in past incidents. This approach is crucial for identifying new threats that utilize previously unencountered IP addresses or domains by observing patterns and behaviors indicative of malicious intent.

Employing both reputational and behavioral threat research methods in tandem offers a comprehensive approach to identifying potential threats, weaving a robust threat research framework that can significantly enhance an organization's security posture.

Engaging in threat research propels security professionals into the intricate and shadowy realm of hacking methodologies and tools. To remain at the forefront of cybersecurity knowledge, a diverse array of research sources should be consulted, including:

Vendor Websites and Vulnerability Feeds: Key for staying informed about the latest security products and vulnerabilities.

Cybersecurity Conferences and Academic Journals: Rich sources of cutting-edge research and discussions on emerging threats.

Request for Comment (RFC) Documents: Technical specifications providing insights into internet and network protocols.

Local Industry Groups and Social Media: Platforms for networking and sharing knowledge with peers.

Threat Feeds and TTP Details: Critical for understanding the evolving tactics, techniques, and procedures of cyber adversaries.

Leveraging a broad spectrum of research sources ensures that cybersecurity professionals are well-equipped with the latest intelligence, ready to counter the dynamic challenges posed by cyber threats.

THREAT IDENTIFICATION

Navigating the complex landscape of cybersecurity threats presents a significant challenge for organizations, making it tough to monitor and discern the most critical risks. Security professionals leverage threat modeling as a strategic method to catalog and prioritize threats, guiding the deployment of appropriate security measures. Rather than adopting a random or unstructured method of brainstorming potential issues—which risks overlooking key threats—a systematic walkthrough of potential dangers is essential.

Three structured strategies can enhance an organization's ability to systematically identify threats:

Asset-Focused Approach: This method starts with a comprehensive review of the organization's asset inventory. Security analysts methodically assess each asset to pinpoint potential threats. For instance, examining the organization's online presence might reveal the risk of internet connectivity disruption due to a severed fiber optic line, impacting website availability.

Threat-Focused Approach: Here, the focus shifts to enumerating various external threats and analyzing their potential impact on organizational systems. By cataloging threats such as cyber attackers, analysts can explore numerous scenarios in which these adversaries might compromise the network. This broad perspective encompasses a range of potential aggressors, from external hackers to internal figures like contractors, partners, or dissatisfied employees, aiming to gauge the adversary's capabilities.

Service-Focused Approach: Particularly relevant for internet service providers, this method involves scrutinizing the services offered, such as public APIs, and assessing the threats specific to each service interface. This approach is instrumental for organizations that deliver digital services, facilitating a targeted analysis of vulnerabilities that could jeopardize those services.

The initial step in threat modeling involves the meticulous identification of all potential threats an organization may face. Adopting one or a combination of these structured approaches ensures a comprehensive and systematic evaluation, laying the groundwork for effective threat prioritization and subsequent security strategy development.

AUTOMATION OF THREAT DETECTIONS

Automation stands out as a transformative force in threat intelligence, offering significant advantages to cybersecurity operations. Here are a few instances where automation can make a substantial difference. A readily implementable security measure is the automated blocking of IP addresses identified by threat intelligence services as origins of malicious activities. These services provide continuously updated feeds of IP addresses, allowing for seamless integration with security devices like firewalls and intrusion prevention systems to block harmful traffic automatically.

The hesitation to implement tools that block traffic without human oversight is understandable due to operational concerns. Thus, organizations are advised to initially set up threat intelligence feeds in a monitoring-only mode. This approach allows cybersecurity teams to scrutinize the potential impact of such blocks, enhancing confidence in the accuracy of these automated systems before fully activating automatic blocking.

Moreover, automation facilitates the consolidation of threat intelligence from various sources into a unified stream, enriching the contextual understanding of potential threats. Another area ripe for automation is incident response, traditionally reliant on manual intervention and the nuanced judgment of security professionals. Automating aspects of incident response, such as gathering preliminary data on incidents, can significantly expedite the initial stages of investigation.

For instance, upon detecting suspicious activity, automated workflows can enrich incident reports with detailed reconnaissance on the source of the attack, including ownership and geolocation of IP addresses, as well as correlating log data and conducting vulnerability scans on affected systems. This preparatory work, executed instantaneously, equips analysts with comprehensive insights, allowing for a more focused review.

Organizations looking to enhance their incident response capabilities should identify repetitive, data-gathering tasks that lend themselves to automation by observing the common practices of their response teams. Security Orchestration, Automation, and Response (SOAR) platforms epitomize the convergence of automation and cybersecurity, streamlining the response process and integrating with existing security technologies for efficient incident management.

The advent of machine learning and artificial intelligence heralds new frontiers for cybersecurity automation. For example, upon the identification of a novel malware variant, analysts can deploy automated tools to generate malware signatures, scanning for distinctive features that inform the creation of signature definition files. This innovative application of technology underscores the potential of automation in crafting agile and robust cybersecurity defenses.

THREAT HUNTING

The cybersecurity landscape has undergone profound changes in recent years. Veterans of the security domain can recall a time when the primary objective was to erect impenetrable defenses to prevent cyber intrusions outright. However, the notion of thwarting every conceivable attack is now viewed as overly optimistic, given the sophistication and resources of contemporary cyber adversaries. This realization has led to a paradigm shift toward what is known as the "assumption of compromise" — the understanding that attackers might already have a presence within our networks, obligating us to proactively seek and neutralize such breaches.

Threat hunting embodies this proactive stance, employing a structured, methodical process to uncover signs of compromise. By leveraging both established security practices and cutting-edge predictive analytics, threat hunters actively patrol for hints of unauthorized activity, diving deep into the data to unearth and investigate anomalies.

The rise in interest in threat hunting is notable, with Google trends indicating a surge in searches post-2016, signifying the widespread adoption of this forward-thinking strategy. Transitioning to threat hunting requires adopting an offensive mindset, essentially thinking like an adversary to anticipate potential breach methods.

Initiating a threat hunting exercise involves formulating a hypothesis based on potential attack vectors, drawing from various sources such as threat actor profiles, threat intelligence feeds, and security advisories. This hypothesis sets the stage for identifying potential indicators of compromise, which could range from the presence of unusual files or processes, atypical system resource usage, unanticipated user accounts or permissions, to anomalies in network traffic, unexplained log entries, or unauthorized configuration changes.

The essence of threat hunting lies in the meticulous search for these indicators, enhancing detection capabilities by integrating internal threat intelligence with external resources and data from security information and event management (SIEM) systems. Highlighting critical assets within analysis tools can expedite the identification of indicators on vital systems.

Upon identifying potential signs of a compromise, the focus shifts to the established incident response protocol, examining the intruder's movement through the network and initiating containment, eradication, and recovery efforts. This proactive approach to cybersecurity represents a significant evolution from purely defensive measures to actively engaging in the hunt for threats, ensuring organizations can better safeguard against the ever-evolving tactics of cyber adversaries.

SOCIAL ENGINEERING

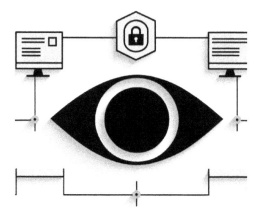

Not all cybersecurity threats stem from digital vulnerabilities; some of the most significant risks involve human psychology. Social engineering stands out as a formidable challenge, leveraging psychological manipulation to breach security measures. For instance, an impostor might impersonate IT support to coax a password out of an unsuspecting employee over the phone. These tactics mirror the deception seen in traditional con games, exploiting human nature to bypass technical defenses.

Social engineering's effectiveness is rooted in six key psychological principles: authority, intimidation, consensus (social proof), scarcity, urgency, and familiarity. Here's a closer examination of each:

Authority: People are naturally inclined to obey figures who exude authority. This could be someone in a suit or simply portraying confidence. Stanley Milgram's experiment highlighted this, showing that participants were willing to administer what they believed were electric shocks to others, under the direction of an authoritative figure. Similarly, hacker Kevin Mitnick recounted a scenario where a social engineer gained access to secure areas simply by acting authoritatively.

Intimidation: This tactic involves coercing compliance through fear, threatening negative consequences for non-cooperation. For example, a social engineer might aggressively demand password resets from help desk personnel, feigning urgency and importance.

Consensus (Social Proof): In uncertain situations, individuals look to others' actions for guidance, a phenomenon known as the herd mentality. Social engineers exploit this by creating scenarios where the target's peers appear to endorse or participate in the desired action.

Scarcity: By suggesting a limited opportunity, attackers can spur targets into hasty actions. This principle is evident in consumer behavior, such as people queuing for the latest gadget release, fearing they might miss out.

Urgency: Creating a false sense of immediacy pressures targets into quick decisions, potentially bypassing usual security protocols. An attacker might pose as a technician needing immediate access to perform urgent repairs, suggesting dire consequences for delay.

Familiarity: People are more likely to comply with requests from someone they like or perceive as friendly. Social engineers employ charm, flattery, and pretended relationships to lower defenses and facilitate their schemes.

To safeguard against social engineering, the key defense is thorough user education. It's essential for everyone within an organization to recognize these manipulation techniques. Training should highlight the importance of vigilance against attempts to exploit the principles of authority, intimidation, consensus, scarcity, urgency, and familiarity. Promoting a culture of skepticism can significantly enhance an organization's resilience against the nuanced threat of social engineering.

IMPERSONATION ATTACKS

Cybersecurity isn't just about guarding against digital attacks; often, the greatest vulnerabilities stem from human behavior. Social engineering exemplifies this challenge, manipulating psychological tendencies to circumvent security protocols. For example, a fraudster might masquerade as a tech support agent to trick an employee into divulging their password. Such strategies echo the manipulative techniques of classic scams, targeting human instincts to sidestep digital safeguards.

Defending against social engineering relies heavily on comprehensive staff training. It's critical that all members of an organization are aware of these manipulation strategies. Educational programs should stress the importance of skepticism towards unsolicited requests or unusual behavior, especially those that tap into the triggers of authority, intimidation, consensus, scarcity, urgency, and familiarity. Cultivating a cautious organizational culture is vital for mitigating the sophisticated threat posed by social engineering.

IDENTITY FRAUD

Identity theft represents a particularly nefarious category of cybercrime, where individuals rather than corporations become the victims. Perpetrators of identity theft seek to impersonate these individuals to illicitly open accounts, misappropriate funds, or conduct other unlawful activities. The Federal Trade Commission (FTC) through its Consumer Sentinel Network, which monitors and compiles data on fraud, identity theft, and similar offenses, reports a significant rise in the incidence of such crimes, evident in their publicly accessible data dashboard.

A common tactic in the arsenal of identity thieves is pretexting. This strategy involves the thief posing as the victim to gain unauthorized access to personal accounts by deceiving third-party companies. Pretexting often serves as an opening gambit in broader schemes of identity theft. For instance, consider a hypothetical scenario where the perpetrator, dubbed "Angry Andy," targets "Naive Norm" with the aim of infiltrating Norm's bank account. Recognizing the challenge of directly cracking Norm's password, Andy investigates and discovers a password reset feature on the bank's website, which necessitates a verification code sent to a pre-registered mobile number.

Initially thwarted due to lack of access to Norm's phone, Andy attempts to persuade Norm's telecom provider to reassign Norm's number to a new device. Failing to answer the provider's security questions, Andy aborts the call. However, a dive into Norm's publicly shared social media content reveals key personal details, enabling Andy to successfully impersonate Norm on a subsequent call, convince the telecom provider to redirect Norm's number to Andy's device, and subsequently gain control over Norm's bank account using the password reset function.

Defending against pretexting attacks is complex, requiring robust security measures at all interaction points. Organizations that interact directly with customers should critically assess their authentication procedures through the lens of potential attackers, identifying and fortifying any vulnerabilities susceptible to pretexting. This proactive approach is vital in safeguarding individuals' identities and preventing the exploitation of personal information.

WATERING HOLE ATTACK

Watering hole attacks are a cunning strategy cybercriminals use to entrap unwary internet users, injecting malware into their devices. Drawing a parallel from the natural world, a watering hole is a vital source of water for animals, especially in arid regions. These spots, while crucial for survival, also present hazards: they can become hotspots for disease transmission and prime hunting grounds for predators awaiting thirsty prey.

In the digital realm, websites act as the modern watering hole, attracting users who place a certain degree of trust in them, akin to approaching a familiar individual rather than an anonymous solicitor. Vulnerabilities in web browsers, along with their extensions and add-ons, frequently become the target of such attacks. Watering hole attacks are a subset of client-side attacks, where the focus is not on exploiting server vulnerabilities but rather those present in the user's browser or client-side software.

One common technique in these attacks involves generating pop-up warnings that many users, through conditioning, dismiss by pressing "Okay," eager to access their desired content. This reflex can be exploited by attackers who embed malware on reputable websites, waiting for visitors to unwittingly trigger the infection. Constructing their own malicious sites isn't a viable strategy for attackers for two reasons: the obvious being the lack of voluntary visitors to a site with overtly malicious intent, and the second being the prevalence of blacklisting—a security measure that blocks access to known harmful sites, thus safeguarding users from self-compromise.

In executing a watering hole attack, the perpetrator first infiltrates a website frequently visited by their target demographic, then selects a client-side exploit capable of breaching the browsers of those visitors. The malware, often including a botnet component, is then surreptitiously placed on the compromised site. The attacker's job becomes a waiting game, anticipating the moment infected systems make contact.

The insidious nature of watering hole attacks stems from their origin on trusted sites, making them a potent vector for targeting specific systems or individuals. Attackers effectively "fish" for their desired victims, who inadvertently come to them. To mitigate the risks associated with watering hole attacks, both web users and website administrators must stay vigilant in applying security updates and patches, ensuring they don't fall prey to these digital predators.

PHYSICAL SOCIAL ENGINEERING

Social engineering doesn't just manifest in the digital realm; attackers often venture into the physical world to execute their schemes. Three common physical techniques include shoulder surfing, dumpster diving, and tailgating.

Shoulder Surfing: This tactic involves the attacker peering over someone's shoulder to spy on sensitive information being entered or viewed on a computer screen. This intrusion might not always be overt; an attacker could subtly observe an individual's laptop screen while seated nearby on public transport. The primary defenses against shoulder surfing are awareness of one's surroundings and the use of privacy screens on devices, which obstruct the view from sideways angles.

Dumpster Diving: In this method, social engineers sift through an organization's discarded documents to find sensitive information. Although uncovering a password might be rare, it's common to find documents that disclose enough about the organization to bolster other forms of social engineering attacks. The simple solution to deter dumpster diving is to shred all documents before disposal, which is both secure and environmentally friendly as shredded paper can still be recycled.

Tailgating: Also known as "piggybacking," this technique exploits courtesy to breach secure areas. An attacker follows closely behind an authorized person entering a secured space, relying on the latter's badge access without having to authenticate themselves. Raising awareness through education and signage can remind individuals to be vigilant against tailgating, enhancing security measures to prevent unauthorized access.

Physical social engineering attacks leverage simplicity for effectiveness, posing a significant threat to organizational security. However, with straightforward preventive measures like the use of privacy screens, document shredding, and heightened awareness, these physical breaches can be significantly mitigated.

ATTACKS

PASSWORD ATTACKS

Passwords are the cornerstone of securing most systems today, offering a fundamental level of protection for a myriad of applications. However, this method is not without its shortcomings. Passwords are susceptible to various forms of attack, with malicious actors devising strategies to crack or steal credentials stored within system files, leading to the compromise of countless user accounts.

In the digital defense playbook, a few physical methodologies stand out for their simplicity and efficacy: shoulder surfing, dumpster diving, and tailgating.

Shoulder Surfing: This straightforward yet invasive method involves an attacker observing a victim's screen to capture sensitive information. While it might conjure images of overt spying, more subtle instances occur in everyday settings, such as peering at a laptop screen on public transport. Countermeasures include heightened situational awareness and the application of screen privacy filters to obscure viewing angles.

Dumpster Diving: The adage "one man's trash is another's treasure" holds true for social engineers who mine discarded documents for confidential data. The likelihood of discovering a direct password might be slim, but unearthed documents can reveal enough about a company to facilitate further breaches. A simple yet effective defense is the comprehensive shredding of all sensitive documents prior to disposal, ensuring they are irrecoverable.

Tailgating: Exploiting the human instinct to be courteous, attackers follow closely behind an authorized individual to gain access to restricted areas without proper authentication. Raising awareness among staff about the dangers of tailgating, coupled with strategic signage, can reinforce the need for vigilance.

These physical approaches to social engineering underscore the blend of simplicity and potential harm they pose to organizational security. Mitigating these risks involves adopting straightforward solutions such as privacy screens, document destruction, and fostering an educated workforce aware of these tactics.

PASSWORD SPRAYING

Two prevalent tactics that exploit weak password practices include password spraying and credential stuffing, presenting significant risks when users fail to adequately safeguard their credentials.

Password Spraying: This technique involves attackers deploying a list of widely-used passwords against numerous accounts simultaneously. An example is leveraging a repository on platforms like GitHub, which might host lists comprising millions of common passwords. Attackers use these lists in broad-strokes attempts to access various accounts, banking on the likelihood that some accounts will have employed these weak passwords. Implementing defenses against password spraying entails integrating these common password lists into the system's access controls, thereby blocking the selection of any too-frequently-used passwords by users.

Credential Stuffing: This attack capitalizes on the tendency of users to recycle their passwords across multiple platforms. When attackers breach a site with lax security and extract user credentials, they can test these credentials on sites with stricter security measures. The underlying assumption for the attackers is that some users will have reused their passwords on several sites. The optimal countermeasure against credential stuffing is encouraging users to utilize unique passwords for each site they visit. Password managers are invaluable tools in this regard, facilitating the creation and management of robust, distinct passwords for every online account. Furthermore, multi-factor authentication (MFA) serves as a robust barrier against both password spraying and credential stuffing by adding an extra layer of security beyond just the password, effectively thwarting attackers even if they manage to guess or obtain the password.

Adopting unique passwords for each account and enabling multi-factor authentication are crucial steps in enhancing security and mitigating the risks posed by these attack strategies.

AI DRIVEN ATTACKS

Machine learning, a field that intersects computer science and statistics, is dedicated to extracting insights from the daily influx of data. By identifying patterns, classifying information, and optimizing business operations, machine learning stands as a critical component of the larger domain of artificial intelligence (AI). AI encompasses a suite of technologies aimed at emulating human cognitive functions in machines, with machine learning being a pivotal element.

In the practice of machine learning, objectives can be broadly categorized into descriptive analytics, predictive analytics, and prescriptive analytics:

Descriptive Analytics focus on providing a snapshot of historical data, offering insights into questions like the demographics of a customer base or patterns in customer behavior.

Predictive Analytics leverage existing datasets to forecast future occurrences. Utilizing historical customer response data, for instance, can inform predictions about future reactions to marketing initiatives, aiding in strategic adjustments to enhance engagement.

Prescriptive Analytics involve the application of simulation and optimization techniques to determine optimal decision-making strategies, such as the ideal allocation of marketing resources or enhancements to manufacturing efficiency.

With the growing reliance on AI within business ecosystems, there emerges a corresponding rise in adversarial AI threats. These threats range from attempts to compromise machine learning algorithms for intellectual property theft, to the corruption of training data, potentially derailing the accuracy and reliability of machine learning models. An alarming manifestation of adversarial AI was demonstrated by McAfee researchers in 2020, who showed that minor alterations to a speed limit sign could deceive an AI algorithm used in autonomous vehicles, such as Tesla's, into misinterpreting the sign's speed limit—a stark illustration of the potential hazards.

As businesses integrate AI more deeply into their operations, acknowledging and preparing for adversarial threats becomes imperative. Developing secure, resilient algorithms to thwart such attacks is not just an option but a necessity in safeguarding the integrity of AI-driven processes.

SQL INJECTION

SQL injection attacks exploit the reliance of many contemporary dynamic web applications on underlying databases for generating dynamic content. For instance, consider a web application employing a basic database-driven authentication system that stores user passwords in a database in plaintext. Upon a user login attempt, the application retrieves the corresponding password from the database and compares it with the input provided by the user. While this approach is not ideal for password authentication, it is commonly employed across numerous websites.

In such scenarios, the web server constructs a query using Structured Query Language (SQL) to request password data from the database. SQL serves as the language utilized by relational databases for creating, updating, deleting, and retrieving data. Although proficiency in writing SQL queries is not necessary for examination purposes, examining examples can aid in comprehending SQL injection attacks.

For example, when the aforementioned web application seeks to retrieve a user's password from the database, it formulates a query comprising a select statement to specify the desired information fields (such as username and password), a from clause to denote the database table containing the relevant data, and a where clause to specify the specific records of interest, typically based on the username provided by the user during login.

However, a hacker may attempt to manipulate this query by inserting malicious input into the username field. For instance, inputting unconventional characters like a single quote, a semicolon, and SQL commands could alter the query's functionality. This altered input may prompt the database to execute unintended commands, potentially compromising security.

To mitigate SQL injection vulnerabilities, two primary techniques can be employed: input validation and parameterized queries. Input validation involves scrutinizing user input to ensure it adheres to expected formats, such as disallowing single quotes that could disrupt SQL queries. Parameterized SQL commands, like stored procedures, store SQL statements on the server, allowing input from applications to be incorporated after processing the SQL, thereby reducing the risk of SQL injection attacks. These approaches bolster security by thwarting attempts to exploit vulnerabilities in SQL queries.

CROSS SITE SCRIPTING

Cross-Site Scripting (XSS) attacks pose significant threats as they can occur surreptitiously without the victim's awareness. These attacks, often abbreviated as XSS, transpire when an assailant injects malevolent code into a third-party website, which subsequently executes within the web browsers of unsuspecting visitors to the site. Let's delve into how these attacks operate.

Webpages are constructed using HTML code, a markup language enabling various advanced formatting options beyond plain text display. HTML permits authors to incorporate diverse elements such as fonts, images, hyperlinks to external sites, and even scripts that execute within visitors' browsers. This functionality is achieved through the utilization of tags. For instance, the B-tag facilitates bold text formatting, the I-tag facilitates italicized text, and the A-tag facilitates hyperlink inclusion. Tags are enclosed within brackets, with an opening tag preceding the content and a closing tag following it, often denoted by a forward slash. For instance, to embolden text, the <b> tag is utilized to begin the bold section, followed by the content, and concluded with </b> to close the bold formatting.

In addition to basic formatting, HTML allows for the inclusion of scripts using the <script> tag, enabling the execution of programs within users' browsers. While scripting is a legitimate tool for enhancing website functionality, in XSS attacks, malevolent actors manipulate legitimate websites into distributing malicious scripts to their users. This often occurs when websites permit users to input content that is then displayed to other users. For instance, online platforms like auction sites may allow users worldwide to post listings. Users may wish to embellish their listings with HTML code to enhance their appearance, potentially including scripts inadvertently. For example, a seller might embed HTML code to display an image of the item being auctioned. However, if malicious HTML containing scripts is injected, it can execute silently in the background, unbeknownst to the user.

Thankfully, defending against XSS attacks is straightforward. Similar to safeguarding against SQL injection attacks, employing input validation on user-supplied HTML input is crucial. Specifically, input validation should scrutinize for attempts to insert script tags and promptly remove any script code from the input to thwart potential XSS threats.

REQUEST FORGERY

Web applications face yet another peril known as cross-site request forgery (CSRF), a threat akin to cross-site scripting attacks but with even graver consequences. Before delving further, it's essential to clarify the terminology surrounding this threat. Cross-site request forgery is often referred to using two distinct acronyms: CSRF or XSRF, while some even opt to pronounce the acronym as "sea surf." However, regardless of the terminology used, all these terms denote the same form of attack.

In contrast to cross-site scripting attacks, which involve injecting malicious scripts into a third-party website's input to be executed by other users' browsers, cross-site request forgery attacks exploit users' simultaneous sessions across multiple open browser tabs. Authenticated sessions persist across different tabs, enabling attackers to manipulate one site to coerce a user's browser into unknowingly issuing unauthorized requests to another site.

To comprehend this authentication mechanism, consider a scenario where a user is logged into multiple sites simultaneously, exemplified by being logged into Google alongside tabs for Wikipedia and Bank of America. Despite opening a new tab and navigating to Google, the user remains authenticated, courtesy of the browser's persistent authentication cookie shared across tabs. While this convenience benefits users by obviating the need for repeated logins, it also renders them vulnerable to cross-site request forgery attacks, akin to cross-site scripting attacks.

Imagine an online payment service that allows account transfers via web requests. An attacker may exploit this by clandestinely coercing users into executing such requests unknowingly. One method involves embedding a fake image tag in a webpage to execute the desired command surreptitiously. For instance, within an online auction site, an innocuous-looking boat sales listing page may harbor an invisible image tag executing an unauthorized bank transfer upon page load, constituting a cross-site request forgery attack.

Mitigating cross-site request forgery attacks poses significant challenges, often necessitating the overhaul of web application architectures to incorporate cryptographically secure tokens in user exchanges. Additionally, strategies include discouraging the use of HTTP GET requests to hinder CSRF attacks, advising users to log out after sessions, and implementing automatic logout mechanisms after idle periods to mitigate CSRF risks.

Notably, while cross-site request forgery primarily targets users, server-side request forgery (SSRF) poses a server-centric variant of this attack. SSRF manipulates server-side application metadata to deceive servers into executing malicious commands or accessing destinations from ostensibly trusted sources, representing a distinct threat vector from CSRF.

OVERFLOW ATTACKS

When developers create applications, they often allocate specific memory segments to store variable data. Users input crucial information into these memory buffers, which the application relies on for its operation. If the developer neglects to verify that the user input fits within the allocated buffer size, a buffer overflow occurs. This can lead to the user's input overflowing from the designated input area into other memory regions, resulting in unpredictable outcomes.

To illustrate this concept, let's consider for example the WebGoat application. Here, we encounter an application managing wifi charges for hotel rooms. We have the ZAP proxy and we navigate through the application. After entering my name and hotel room number and submitting the form, I inspect the intercepted request in the ZAP proxy. The application then proceeds to a second page, prompting me to accept the pricing plan. Upon inspection in the proxy, we notice that our name and room number are stored in hidden fields, even though they weren't visible on the previous page—a curious observation.

Now, let's restart the application and attempt a buffer overflow attack. Assuming the developers haven't imposed any limits on the room number input field, I input an excessively long room number—4,097 digits, to be precise. Upon submitting the form again and inspecting the request in the proxy, I notice that the application is about to process the exceedingly long room number. Upon confirmation, I observe my name and the lengthy room number in the results. However, upon further examination, I discover that the application has also included the names and room numbers of all other hotel guests.

This demonstrates how a buffer overflow, specifically an integer overflow, can lead to unexpected behavior. By inputting an excessively long room number, I inadvertently accessed information about other hotel guests. This issue could have been mitigated with simple input validation, such as limiting room numbers to a reasonable length.

SESSION HIJACKING ATTACK

Session hijacking, also known as session fixation, is a type of cyber attack where an attacker seizes control of a user's active session on a computer system or web application. The goal of session hijacking is to gain unauthorized access to the user's account or sensitive information.

Here's how a session hijacking attack typically occurs:

Session Establishment: When a user logs into a website or application, a session is established between the user's browser and the server. During this process, the server assigns a unique session identifier (session ID) to the user, which is stored as a cookie in the user's browser.

Session Hijacking: The attacker intercepts the communication between the user's browser and the server, usually by eavesdropping on the network traffic. This can be achieved through various means such as packet sniffing, man-in-the-middle (MitM) attacks, or exploiting vulnerabilities in the network or application layer.

Session ID Capture: Once the attacker intercepts the session ID, they can use it to impersonate the legitimate user and gain access to their active session. The attacker may also try to guess or brute force session IDs to hijack sessions.

Session Manipulation: With control of the session, the attacker can perform various malicious actions, including:

Accessing the user's account and sensitive information.

Conducting unauthorized transactions or actions on behalf of the user.

Modifying or deleting data within the user's session.

Performing actions that the user has privileges for, such as changing account settings or passwords.

Maintaining Control: To prolong their control over the hijacked session, the attacker may use techniques such as session fixation (where they force the user to use a session ID of their choice) or session resurrection (where they re-use a previously captured session ID).

Session hijacking attacks can have serious consequences, leading to data breaches, financial loss, identity theft, and reputational damage for individuals and organizations. To prevent session hijacking, it's essential to implement robust security measures such as:

Using secure HTTPS connections to encrypt data transmitted between the user's browser and the server.

Employing strong session management practices, including regularly rotating session IDs and implementing session timeouts.

Implementing multi-factor authentication (MFA) to add an extra layer of security beyond username and password authentication.

Monitoring network traffic and detecting and blocking suspicious activities that may indicate a session hijacking attempt.

Keeping web applications and software up to date with security patches to mitigate vulnerabilities that attackers could exploit.

CODE EXECUTION ATTACKS

Code execution attacks represent a distinct category of cyber assaults wherein the perpetrator exploits a weakness within a system, enabling them to execute commands on said system. Numerous avenues exist through which an attacker may establish this foothold, typically exploiting resources exposed by the target system to the outside world. For instance, a publicly accessible web server must expose ports 80 and/or 443, facilitating access to the server software, such as Apache or Microsoft IIS. Upon discovering a code execution vulnerability within this web server software, an attacker may exploit the flaw on an unpatched server, enabling them to execute commands of their choosing on the system. This scenario, where an attacker wields the ability to run arbitrary commands, is referred to as arbitrary code execution. If this occurs remotely, it is termed remote code execution.

Perpetrators leveraging code execution vulnerabilities possess the capability to execute any desired action on the targeted system. Should they deceive a process into executing their code with administrative privileges, they attain unrestricted access to the system. Potential actions undertaken by an attacker include deploying malicious code, integrating the system into a botnet, pilfering sensitive data, or establishing accounts for future system access.

To safeguard systems against code execution attacks, two fundamental measures can be adopted. Firstly, when such attacks occur within an application running on a server, the executed code operates within the confines of that application process. Therefore, it is prudent to restrict access by running application services with limited accounts adhering to the principle of least privilege. This mitigates the impact of a successful code execution attack. Secondly, code execution attacks typically exploit vulnerabilities within applications or operating systems, many of which have known patches. Maintaining up-to-date patches for both operating systems and applications is a crucial and effective security practice.

For instance, in March 2020, Microsoft issued a security bulletin addressing a remote code execution vulnerability within Microsoft Windows, particularly within the Server Message Block (SMB) protocol. Exploitation of this vulnerability against a server involves sending it a specially crafted packet, or against a Windows client through a malicious SMB server. Thankfully, a patch is available to rectify this vulnerability. By implementing these straightforward measures - restricting the usage of administrative accounts and applying security updates - systems can be shielded against code execution vulnerabilities.

PRIVILEGE ESCALATION

Privilege escalation is a cybersecurity attack that involves an unauthorized user or attacker attempting to gain elevated access or privileges within a system or network. This means moving from a lower level of access, typically associated with a regular user account, to a higher level of access, such as an administrative or privileged account.

There are two main types of privilege escalation:

Horizontal Privilege Escalation: In this type, an attacker with limited access attempts to gain access to another user's account with similar privileges. For example, an attacker may try to compromise another user's credentials to gain access to their account on the same level of access.

Vertical Privilege Escalation: Here, the attacker aims to escalate their privileges from a lower-level account to a higher-level account, such as gaining administrative privileges. This can be achieved through various means, including exploiting vulnerabilities in software, misconfigurations, or abusing trust relationships.

Privilege escalation attacks can be particularly dangerous because they grant attackers greater control over a system or network, allowing them to execute malicious actions, access sensitive data, install malware, or make unauthorized changes to system configurations.

Mitigating privilege escalation attacks involves implementing security measures such as:

- Employing the principle of least privilege, which ensures that users have only the minimum level of access required to perform their tasks.
- Regularly patching and updating systems and applications to address known vulnerabilities.
- Implementing strong authentication mechanisms, such as multi-factor authentication, to prevent unauthorized access to accounts.
- Monitoring user activities and system logs for suspicious behavior that may indicate an attempted privilege escalation.

- Conducting regular security audits and assessments to identify and remediate any security weaknesses or misconfigurations that could be exploited by attackers.

By implementing these security practices, organizations can reduce the risk of privilege escalation attacks and better protect their systems and data from unauthorized access and misuse.

It is imperative for software developers to ensure that their code is resistant to privilege escalation attacks, which aim to elevate regular user accounts to administrative status. Such attacks pose significant risks, particularly on systems exposed to external threats, potentially enabling unauthorized individuals on the internet to gain control over a server. Privilege escalation vulnerabilities commonly stem from issues like buffer overflows or other security flaws in the code, which allow end users to execute arbitrary commands on the server. Once an end user gains access to the underlying operating system, they exploit these vulnerabilities to escalate their privileges to administrative levels.

To mitigate the risk of successful privilege escalation attacks, developers and operations teams can implement several fundamental strategies. Firstly, developers should conduct thorough input validation on all user-provided inputs, rigorously checking for expected formats and appropriate lengths. Secondly, operations teams must ensure that servers run on up-to-date and supported versions of operating systems, platforms, and applications, incorporating all available security patches. Thirdly, developers and system engineers should collaborate to adhere to the principle of least privilege, assigning only the minimum necessary privileges to service accounts supporting code execution. Granting excessive privileges to these accounts can amplify the impact of an attacker exploiting the code. Lastly, IT organizations should utilize dedicated controls such as Data Execution Prevention and Address Space Layout Randomization technologies to thwart privilege escalation attempts.

By adopting these straightforward measures, organizations can significantly enhance code security and effectively thwart privilege escalation attacks.

BRUTE FORCE ATTACKS

Throughout the history of cybersecurity, encryption has been utilized to safeguard sensitive data, yet adversaries have persistently attempted to subvert this protection and illicitly access information. Over time, attackers have devised various methods to undermine cryptographic algorithms. Brute-force attacks represent the most straightforward approach to assaulting a cryptographic system. In a brute-force attack, the assailant repetitively guesses the encryption key until stumbling upon the correct value, thus gaining entry to the encrypted data. Naturally, guessing proves challenging, and brute-force attacks can span extended durations or even fail altogether. These attacks necessitate minimal information to commence, typically requiring only a sample of encrypted text, earning them the moniker of known ciphertext attacks.

For instance, a shift of one transforms 'A's into 'B's, 'B's into 'C's, and so forth. Similarly, with a shift of three, 'A's become 'D's, 'B's become 'E's, and so on. This cipher is simplistic, offering only 25 possible keys. Shifting the letters by 26 positions results in unchanged ciphertext, demonstrating a small keyspace where there are merely 25 distinct encryption keys. An individual executing a brute-force attack would need to attempt at most 25 guesses before deciphering the key.

However, modern algorithms typically resist brute-force attacks. Consider the data encryption standard, which utilizes a mere 56-bit key, offering 72 quadrillion potential combinations, thereby making key guessing exceedingly difficult. For instance, an advanced encryption standard with a 128-bit key presents an astronomical number of possibilities. Nonetheless, if a cryptographic system possesses a flaw that restricts the keyspace due to a weak implementation, brute-force attacks may exploit this vulnerability.

DENIAL OF SERVICE ATTACKS

A Denial-of-Service (DoS) attack is a malicious attempt to disrupt the normal functioning of a targeted server, service, or network by overwhelming it with a flood of illegitimate traffic, requests, or data. The primary objective of a DoS attack is to render the target inaccessible to legitimate users, causing disruption or complete downtime of the services provided by the target.

There are various types and techniques of DoS attacks, each with its own characteristics and methods of execution. Some of the most common DoS attack types include:

Ping Flood: In a ping flood attack, the attacker sends a large number of ICMP Echo Request (ping) packets to the target server or network. This flood of ping packets overwhelms the target's network capacity and consumes its resources, resulting in network congestion and potential downtime.

SYN Flood: SYN flood attacks exploit the TCP three-way handshake process. The attacker sends a large number of TCP SYN (synchronize) packets to the target server, but does not complete the handshake process by sending the final ACK (acknowledge) packet. This causes the target server to allocate resources for incomplete connections, eventually exhausting its capacity to accept legitimate connections and leading to denial of service.

UDP Flood: UDP flood attacks target the User Datagram Protocol (UDP), flooding the target with a large volume of UDP packets. Unlike TCP, UDP is connectionless and does not require a handshake process, making it easier to flood a target with UDP traffic. This type of attack can overwhelm the target's network infrastructure and disrupt services that rely on UDP, such as DNS or VoIP.

HTTP Flood: HTTP flood attacks target web servers by sending a large number of HTTP requests to the target website or web application. These requests may appear legitimate at first glance, but they are generated by automated scripts or botnets, aiming to exhaust the target server's resources (such as CPU, memory, or bandwidth) and cause it to become unresponsive or slow to respond to legitimate user requests.

Application Layer Attacks: Application layer attacks, also known as Layer 7 attacks, target specific vulnerabilities in web applications or services. These attacks often involve sending specially crafted requests to exploit weaknesses in the target application's code or logic. Examples include HTTP POST floods, slowloris attacks, and XML/SOAP attacks.

Mitigating DoS attacks requires a combination of proactive measures and reactive responses:

Network Security: Implementing network security measures such as firewalls, intrusion detection/prevention systems (IDS/IPS), and rate limiting can help mitigate the impact of DoS attacks by filtering and blocking malicious traffic.

Traffic Filtering: Utilizing traffic filtering techniques, such as access control lists (ACLs) or IP blacklisting, can help identify and block malicious traffic sources, reducing the impact of DoS attacks on the network.

Load Balancing: Distributing incoming traffic across multiple servers using load balancers can help distribute the load and prevent any single server from being overwhelmed by a DoS attack.

Anomaly Detection: Deploying anomaly detection systems that monitor network traffic patterns and behavior can help identify and mitigate DoS attacks in real-time by detecting abnormal traffic spikes or patterns indicative of an attack.

Content Delivery Networks (CDNs): Leveraging CDNs can help mitigate the impact of DoS attacks by caching and delivering content closer to end-users, reducing the load on origin servers and providing additional layers of protection against DDoS attacks.

Incident Response: Developing and implementing incident response plans that outline procedures for detecting, analyzing, and mitigating DoS attacks can help minimize downtime and restore services quickly in the event of an attack.

Overall, defending against DoS attacks requires a comprehensive approach that combines technical controls, network monitoring, and incident response capabilities to mitigate the impact and ensure the availability and integrity of critical systems and services.

EAVESDROPPING

If a malicious actor gains physical or logical access to a network, they could potentially intercept communications between two systems on that network, posing a significant threat. This becomes especially concerning if the attacker is able to decrypt encrypted communications, granting them access to confidential information without the knowledge or consent of the parties involved. All eavesdropping attacks necessitate some form of compromise to the communication path between a client and a server. This could involve intercepting network devices or cables, or executing DNS or ARP poisoning attacks to redirect traffic to the attacker rather than its intended destination.

Before delving into various eavesdropping attacks, it's important to understand the basics of web communications. When a user initiates a connection to a server via a web browser, the communication traverses multiple network connections. Each intermediary device along the route presents an opportunity for eavesdropping. Encryption protocols like HTTPS help safeguard against simple eavesdropping by preventing intermediaries from viewing or tampering with the communication.

However, attackers can employ more sophisticated techniques like the man-in-the-middle (MitM) attack to circumvent encryption. In a MitM attack, the attacker deceives the sending system during the initial communication setup, often through network reconfiguration or DNS/ARP poisoning. Consequently, the user unknowingly establishes a connection with the attacker posing as the legitimate server. Acting as a relay, the attacker intercepts and can inspect all communications between the client and the server, relaying them back and forth without detection.

A variant of the MitM attack, known as a man-in-the-browser (MitB) attack, involves compromising the user's web browser or browser plugin to intercept web communications. Both MitM and MitB attacks are classified as on-path attacks since the attacker positions themselves along the communication path between the user and the service.

Furthermore, if attackers can capture network traffic, they may execute replay attacks. In a replay attack, previously captured data like encrypted authentication tokens are reused to establish a fraudulent connection with the server. To mitigate replay attacks, secure protocols often employ session tokens or timestamps. Session tokens are randomly generated and have a limited lifespan, rendering replayed tokens invalid. Timestamps ensure that packets are sent within a specific timeframe, preventing replay attacks beyond that window.

Lastly, SSL stripping is another variation of eavesdropping attacks where an attacker manipulates a user's browser to revert from encrypted to unencrypted communications, allowing them to intercept and view sensitive information. This process effectively removes the SSL or TLS protection from the communication, making it vulnerable to interception.

DNS ATTACKS

DNS (Domain Name System) attacks are a type of cyber attack that target the Domain Name System, which is responsible for translating human-readable domain names into machine-readable IP addresses. These attacks exploit vulnerabilities or weaknesses in the DNS infrastructure to disrupt or manipulate the process of domain name resolution, causing various adverse effects. Here are some common types of DNS attacks:

DNS Spoofing or DNS Cache Poisoning: In this attack, the attacker falsifies DNS information stored in the cache of a DNS resolver. By sending forged DNS responses to the resolver, the attacker can redirect users to malicious websites or intercept their traffic. This can lead users to unknowingly interact with fraudulent sites or expose sensitive information to attackers.

DNS Amplification Attack: This type of attack involves sending a large number of DNS queries with spoofed source IP addresses to open DNS resolvers. The resolvers then respond to the forged IP addresses, flooding the victim's network with an overwhelming volume of DNS responses. This can lead to network congestion, service disruption, or even a distributed denial-of-service (DDoS) attack.

DNS Tunneling: DNS tunneling involves encoding data within DNS queries and responses to bypass network security measures. Attackers use DNS tunnels to exfiltrate data from a compromised network or to establish covert communication channels with command and control servers. This technique allows attackers to evade detection and transfer sensitive information stealthily.

DNS Hijacking: DNS hijacking occurs when attackers gain unauthorized access to DNS settings or credentials, allowing them to modify DNS records for legitimate domains. By redirecting domain names to malicious IP addresses, attackers can intercept traffic intended for legitimate websites, steal credentials, or distribute malware to unsuspecting users.

Distributed Reflection Denial-of-Service (DRDoS) Attack: In this type of attack, the attacker exploits misconfigured DNS servers to amplify and reflect DNS traffic towards the victim's network. By spoofing the source IP address of the DNS queries, the attacker can amplify the volume of traffic directed at the victim, overwhelming their network resources and causing service disruption.

Mitigating DNS attacks requires implementing robust security measures, such as:

DNSSEC (Domain Name System Security Extensions): DNSSEC adds cryptographic authentication to DNS responses, preventing DNS spoofing and ensuring the integrity of DNS data.

DNS Filtering: Employing DNS filtering solutions can help block access to malicious domains and prevent users from accessing known malicious websites.

DNS Monitoring and Logging: Regularly monitoring DNS traffic and logging DNS activities can help detect suspicious behavior and identify potential attacks in real-time.

Regular Software Patching and Updates: Keeping DNS servers and network devices up-to-date with the latest security patches and updates helps mitigate vulnerabilities that could be exploited by attackers.

Implementing Rate Limiting and Access Controls: Configuring rate-limiting measures and access controls on DNS servers can help prevent DNS amplification attacks and limit the impact of abusive DNS queries.

By understanding the various types of DNS attacks and implementing appropriate security measures, organizations can better protect their DNS infrastructure and mitigate the risks associated with DNS vulnerabilities.

WIRELESS ATTACKS

As a cybersecurity professional, it's essential to grasp the various choices available for Wi-Fi encryption and comprehend the inherent insecurity of the Wired Equivalent Privacy (WEP) protocol. Let's delve deeper into this and explore how attackers could exploit a WEP network. During the setup of a new WEP connection, there's an exchange of an initialization vector (IV) between the computer and access point to facilitate connection establishment. This IV transmission occurs without encryption because it's utilized to form the encrypted channel. If an attacker manages to capture a sufficient number of different initialization vectors, they can reconstruct the encryption key employed for the web connection. While the intricate mathematical workings behind this attack might be complex, it's crucial to grasp that WEP attacks hinge on capturing initialization vectors.

Wi-Fi Protected Access (WPA), similar to WEP, relies on the RC4 encryption standard. However, the issue with WEP lies in the fact that hackers monitoring the network over an extended period can accumulate enough plaintext information to deduce the unchanging encryption key. WPA introduces a novel aspect to WEP through the Temporal Key Integrity Protocol (TKIP), ensuring that the encryption key changes continuously. With TKIP, each packet sent across the network undergoes a change in the encryption key, thwarting any attempts by attackers to accumulate a significant volume of traffic encrypted with the same key.

Yet, is WPA completely secure? Unfortunately, it's not. Attackers have identified vulnerabilities in a hashing function utilized by WPA, rendering it insecure as well. In essence, to err on the side of caution, opt for WPA2 or WPA3 if feasible. These standards eschew TKIP, thus circumventing this problem. To date, researchers have not unearthed any notable security vulnerabilities in WPA2 or WPA3.

Let's now shift our focus to another wireless security concern revolving around Wi-Fi Protected Setup (WPS). WPS aims to simplify the process of connecting new devices to a wireless network, particularly in residential settings. When employing Wi-Fi Protected Setup to link a new device, users are presented with two options: they can either press a WPS button on both devices for automatic connection establishment or utilize an eight-digit WPS PIN. At first glance, this may seem secure, considering there are 11 million potential PIN combinations, making it a time-consuming task to guess them all. However, cryptographers have uncovered a mathematical flaw in the WPS algorithm, rendering the PIN easily guessable. Attackers can ascertain a WPS PIN with just 11,000 attempts. Once the PIN is obtained, determining the encryption key becomes effortless, granting access to all network communications. Adding to the predicament is the inability to alter the WPS PIN on a device. While WPS isn't commonly found on enterprise-grade Wi-Fi access points, should it be encountered, it's imperative to promptly disable this technology.

PROPAGATION ATTACKS

Propagation attacks refer to malicious activities aimed at spreading malware or malicious content from one system to another within a network or across networks. These attacks often exploit vulnerabilities in software or systems to gain access and then proliferate throughout the network, infecting other connected devices. Propagation attacks can take various forms, such as email attachments containing malware, infected websites distributing malicious code, or worms exploiting network vulnerabilities to self-replicate and infect other devices. The goal of propagation attacks is to rapidly spread the malicious payload across a wide range of systems, maximizing the attacker's impact and control over the compromised network.

ROGUES AND EVIL TWINS

Rogue access points manifest when an individual connects an unauthorized wireless access point to an enterprise network. This could range from a scenario where an employee, facing poor wireless connectivity in their workspace, procures an access point and plugs it into a network port to improve their signal strength, to a more malicious situation where a hacker sets up an access point with the intention of later infiltrating the network remotely. The significant danger posed by rogue access points lies in their ability to circumvent other wireless authentication mechanisms. Even if extensive effort is devoted to configuring systems to utilize WPA3 security, a rogue access point configured to bypass encryption can swiftly evade these measures. Users connecting to the rogue access point can consequently obtain unrestricted entry into the network. Another peril associated with rogue access points is interference. With only a limited number of available WiFi channels, rogue access points can swiftly disrupt legitimate wireless operations.

IT personnel should vigilantly monitor their premises and network environments for the presence of rogue access points and promptly disable them upon detection. Various technologies can aid in this endeavor. For instance, enterprise-grade wireless networks often feature built-in wireless intrusion detection systems. These systems enable access points to detect unknown access points within their vicinity and provide a rough estimate of the rogue access point's location through triangulation. By leveraging signal strength and direction data from multiple legitimate access points, IT staff can approximate the general location of the rogue access point. Subsequently, personnel responding to this location can employ handheld devices to pinpoint the precise location of the rogue device and disconnect it from the network. Notably, during the Super Bowl, National Football League staff utilized this technology to identify fans whose smartphones' personal hotspot features were causing interference with stadium wireless networks.

Evil twin attacks, akin to phishing and farming attacks, represent a related threat. In such attacks, a hacker establishes a counterfeit access point with the SSID matching that of a legitimate network. Unsuspecting users, upon entering the vicinity, automatically connect to this fraudulent network. As the hacker controls the network, they can employ tactics like

DNS poisoning to redirect users to phishing websites. Executing an evil twin attack becomes straightforward when attackers utilize common SSIDs to which millions of computers are preconfigured to connect automatically. Through tools such as the Karma toolkit, attackers can automate evil twin attacks by identifying legitimate networks nearby, creating counterfeit networks, and setting up bogus websites to capture user credentials.

Enterprises must implement robust controls to swiftly detect and eradicate rogue access points from their networks. Furthermore, educating users about the risks associated with connecting to unknown open access points without utilizing a VPN connection is imperative.

KNOWLEDGE BASED ATTACKS

Knowledge-based attacks transcend the simplicity of brute-force attacks by integrating additional information available to the attacker with cryptanalytic techniques to compromise the security of encrypted data. The foremost knowledge-based attack is the frequency analysis attack, where the attacker conducts statistical analysis of the ciphertext to identify patterns. Utilizing common characteristics of the English language aids in this analysis. For instance, recognizing that the most frequent letters in English are E, T, O, A, I, and N can suggest potential substitutions in a simple substitution cipher. Moreover, lesser-known rules, such as analyzing pairs of letters known as digraphs, can further assist in deciphering the text. These rules facilitate frequency analysis by identifying recurring patterns in the ciphertext.

While detailed proficiency in these techniques may not be required, understanding the concept of frequency analysis and its application in deciphering ciphertext is crucial. Additionally, in some scenarios, cryptanalysts may possess both the encrypted and unencrypted versions of a message, enabling a known plaintext attack. This attack leverages the known information to decrypt other messages by deducing the decryption key. Furthermore, cryptanalysts may gain a strategic advantage by encrypting a message using the designated algorithm and key, enabling a chosen plaintext attack. In this attack, the adversary scrutinizes the algorithm's operations to deduce the utilized key.

The birthday attack is another knowledge-based attack that seeks potential collisions in a hash function, allowing attackers to exploit the function's vulnerabilities. The term "Birthday attack" originates from the Birthday Problem, a mathematical quandary illustrating the probability of individuals in a group sharing the same birth month and day. As depicted in the chart, the likelihood of such shared birthdays increases exponentially with the group size. For instance, with 23 people, there's a 50% chance of two individuals sharing a birthday, rising to near certainty with 70 people.

VULNERABILITIES IN DEPTH

TYPES OF VULNERABILITIES

Our digital infrastructure, systems, and applications are often riddled with vulnerabilities that can potentially lead to security incidents. Before delving into these vulnerabilities, it's crucial to understand the core objectives of cybersecurity and the variety of risks organizations may encounter.

A commonly referenced framework in cybersecurity is the CIA triad, which outlines the three foundational goals of information security within an organization: confidentiality, integrity, and availability.

Confidentiality is about ensuring that information is accessible only to those who are authorized. This aspect of cybersecurity is what most people initially think of—safeguarding sensitive information from unauthorized access. The main challenge here is preventing the disclosure of sensitive data without the owner's consent, often referred to as a data breach or data exfiltration when information is illicitly removed from a network.

Integrity involves maintaining the accuracy and reliability of data, guarding against unauthorized modifications. These could stem from deliberate actions by malicious actors or inadvertent disruptions that affect data stored in systems. It's the job of cybersecurity professionals to safeguard against these threats to data integrity.

Availability ensures that authorized users have reliable access to information and resources when needed. Disruptions in availability can have significant operational impacts. Denial of service attacks, which aim to incapacitate a system or network, are common tactics used to undermine this aspect of security.

The ramifications of a security incident can vary widely, affecting organizations in multiple ways:

Financial Risk involves the potential for monetary losses resulting from a security incident. This might encompass costs related to recovery efforts, incident investigations, or the ramifications of compromised data leading to identity theft for individuals.

Reputational Risk arises from the negative perception following a security breach, potentially eroding trust among customers, employees, and partners. Although challenging to quantify, the loss of goodwill can have long-term impacts on business relationships and customer loyalty.

Strategic Risk refers to the potential hindrance to achieving key organizational objectives due to a security breach. An example could be the loss of confidential product development plans, which could delay product launches or advantage competitors.

Operational Risk is the threat to daily business operations, possibly slowing down processes, delaying customer orders, or necessitating manual interventions for typically automated tasks.

Compliance Risk occurs when a security breach leads to violations of legal or regulatory standards, such as HIPAA in the healthcare sector. Non-compliance can result in legal penalties and fines.

In conducting a vulnerability analysis, it's vital to consider these diverse risk categories and evaluate the potential impacts of exploited vulnerabilities on the organization.

SUPPLY CHAIN VULNERABILITIES

IT departments universally rely on a mix of hardware, software, and services procured from third-party vendors, ranging from server OS and databases to managed services and applications. It's crucial for IT administrators to grasp how supply chain security vulnerabilities might affect their operations. A key concern is monitoring vendors' end-of-life (EOL) announcements for products in use, as these signify the cessation of patch support, exposing systems to unresolved security vulnerabilities.

Understanding End-of-Life Terminology

The terminology around product EOL varies across vendors, but there are three commonly used terms indicating a product's lifecycle phase:

End-of-Sale (EOS) marks the point where a vendor stops selling the product but continues supporting existing customers.

End-of-Support (EOS) signals when a vendor will halt certain levels of support, which might range from stopping non-security related updates to ceasing all enhancements. The specifics of an EOS announcement are vital for understanding the potential impact on your infrastructure.

End-of-Life (EOL) is the final phase where a vendor discontinues all support, including security patches, and generally ceases to respond to support queries, focusing instead on assisting customers with upgrading to newer product versions.

Staying informed about the support status of all vendor-supplied products is essential for maintaining a secure IT environment. For instance, Cisco maintains a consolidated webpage detailing all its products' EOS and EOL announcements.

Unplanned Vendor Support Issues

Apart from structured EOL processes, vendors might fail to offer sufficient support due to resource limitations or a lack of commitment, posing risks akin to using unsupported products but harder to identify. This risk is amplified when vendor systems are part of a broader operational framework, including embedded systems that users cannot directly update. For example, a digital signage system running on an unseen Linux version becomes vulnerable if that Linux version is compromised, with updates depending on the vendor's responsiveness.

Cloud Services and Vendor Dependency

Relying on vendors for cloud services shifts some responsibility for risk management to the vendor, necessitating trust in their commitment to security. Additionally, the longevity and reliability of the vendor become concerns, especially for services like data storage, where losing access to data could be catastrophic. A potential mitigation strategy involves maintaining backups in a secondary, vendor-independent environment.

In today's IT landscape, vendor reliance is inevitable, but cybersecurity professionals must diligently oversee these relationships to safeguard their organizations' operational security.

CONFIGURATION VULNERABILITIES

Misconfigurations in system settings can significantly endanger an organization's cybersecurity. Simple oversights in configuring a system can open up major security vulnerabilities, potentially allowing attackers to access or compromise sensitive data and systems. A frequent mistake by IT personnel is deploying devices with their factory settings intact on the network, a practice that's particularly risky for devices with embedded computers not traditionally monitored by IT, such as printers, building management systems, and lab equipment. These devices might arrive with insecure default settings, including poorly configured firewalls, open ports, default user accounts and passwords, and unsecured administrative access, all of which pose substantial security threats.

To ensure the security of these devices, IT teams must rigorously inspect and adjust the settings of all equipment before integration into the network. The complexity of system, application, and device configurations means that even minor mistakes can create major security gaps, potentially giving attackers unfettered access to the network. Adhering to established security guidelines and configuration benchmarks is vital for securely setting up systems.

Misconfigured cryptographic protocols present another hazard. Incorrect settings, such as enabling weak encryption methods, can make sensitive communications vulnerable to interception and tampering. Such errors could stem from as simple an action as selecting the wrong option in a setup menu. Moreover, the secure management of encryption keys is paramount; a compromised key can lead to unauthorized impersonation and data breaches. Similarly, the issuance and management of digital certificates require stringent controls to prevent abuse and protect associated private keys.

Patch management plays a crucial role in maintaining system security, addressing vulnerabilities through updates from manufacturers. While operating system updates are often prioritized, it's essential not to overlook patches for applications and firmware on various devices. An unpatched component can serve as a gateway for attackers to infiltrate the network.

Account management also demands careful attention. Accounts granted more permissions than necessary can be exploited, either maliciously by insiders or inadvertently by uninformed users. Upholding the principle of least privilege—limiting user permissions to the bare minimum needed for their role—helps mitigate this risk.

In summary, the diligent configuration of systems, devices, applications, and user accounts, guided by the principle of least privilege, is indispensable in fortifying an organization's defense against cyber threats.

VULNERABLE ARCHITECTURES

Architectural vulnerabilities emerge from flaws in the initial design of complex systems, leading to inherent security gaps that are challenging to address later on. IT architecture involves structured methodologies and processes for constructing intricate technical solutions, with IT architects playing a crucial role akin to that of building architects, but with a focus on integrating diverse technologies to fulfill organizational needs, among which security stands paramount.

The cornerstone of crafting secure architectures and system designs lies in embedding security considerations from the outset as fundamental design elements, rather than retrofitting them as an afterthought. A common pitfall is developing a system's structure first with the intention of adding security features subsequently, which often leads to compromised security.

Assessing the security of a system extends beyond its technical framework to encompass the associated business processes and human factors. For instance, a system that encrypts data effectively may still be compromised if the operational workflow results in sensitive information being printed and left unguarded, exposing it to potential breaches. The human element—untrained personnel and lax business procedures—can significantly undermine the security infrastructure.

With the continuous expansion of networked systems and devices within organizations, a phenomenon referred to as system sprawl emerges. This sprawl involves the accumulation of devices that, while initially essential, become obsolete yet remain connected to the network, often without adequate documentation, maintenance, or security updates. This neglect creates vulnerabilities within the network's defenses.

To mitigate these risks, security professionals must evaluate their organization's architectural and operational practices, ensuring the integration of robust security measures. This proactive approach is key to building a resilient and secure IT infrastructure.

VULNERABILITY SCANNING

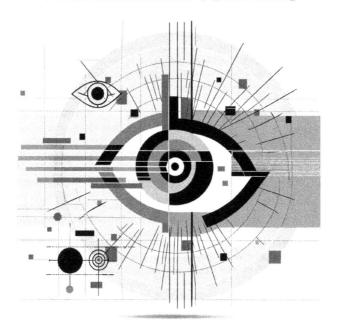

Today's computing landscapes and software applications are intricately complex. It's a common fact that major software applications encompass millions of lines of code. Take, for instance, the Linux kernel, which lies at the heart of the Linux operating system, managing critical tasks like input/output processing, memory, and CPU management. This essential component comprises over 24 million lines of code, with thousands more being modified, added, or removed daily as it continues to evolve. This level of complexity makes it a given that developers will occasionally err, leading to potential security vulnerabilities.

The security sector has established a systematic approach to handling such vulnerabilities. Upon identifying a vulnerability, a company will assess the problem, devise a solution or patch, and distribute this patch via their updating systems. System administrators worldwide then apply these patches to mitigate the identified security risk.

The task of managing these vulnerabilities can be daunting. An average enterprise might utilize multiple operating systems, numerous applications, and a wide array of devices and software components, all needing regular updates and patches. This is where the necessity for a comprehensive vulnerability management strategy comes into play, involving system scanning for vulnerabilities, patch application, tracking remediations, and compiling reports on the findings.

Embarking on creating a vulnerability management plan requires a clear understanding of the objectives behind it. While the primary goal is to enhance system security, there could be other driving factors, such as compliance with company policies or external regulations that mandate specific vulnerability management practices. For example, adherence to the Payment Card Industry Data Security Standard (PCI DSS) for entities handling credit card data entails stringent vulnerability scanning requirements. Similarly, U.S. government agencies must conform to the Federal Information Security Management Act (FISMA), following detailed security control guidelines provided in NIST Special Publication 800-53, including regular vulnerability assessments and remediations.

Developing a vulnerability management program also involves integrating different types of vulnerability assessments—network scans, application scans, and specialized web application tests—to identify a broad spectrum of potential security issues. It's crucial to remember that vulnerability scanning is just one part of a larger security assessment strategy, which should also include configuration and log reviews to ensure accuracy and identify any discrepancies in the scan results.

Regardless of the reasons for establishing a vulnerability management program, the fundamental tools and methodologies remain consistent. However, it's vital to first comprehend the specific requirements and regulations applicable to your organization to ensure the program meets all necessary criteria.

SCANNING TARGETS

Launching a vulnerability management program begins with defining its objectives. These objectives might stem from a desire to bolster security, adhere to regulatory standards, or align with corporate guidelines. Once the purpose is clear, the next task is to specify which systems and networks require scanning. This necessitates a reliable asset inventory, a foundational tool for effective vulnerability management.

For organizations with robust asset management practices, an existing inventory might already be in place, possibly detailed within configuration management tools or kept current through routine network discovery scans. In cases where such a comprehensive inventory isn't available, initiating a preliminary scan with your vulnerability management tool can help identify networked systems. These preliminary scans, aimed at detecting systems rather than probing for vulnerabilities, provide a foundational understanding of the network's scope without the exhaustive process of a full vulnerability scan.

Examples using the Nessus scanner will illustrate how to conduct various types of scans, starting with basic host discovery. Setting up a host discovery scan in Nessus, for example, involves naming the scan, specifying scan targets—like a range of private IP addresses—and launching the scan to compile a list of network hosts. This list serves as a starting point for more in-depth vulnerability assessments.

With an asset inventory in hand, prioritization becomes the focus. Prioritizing assets for scanning typically involves evaluating three main factors:

The Asset's Importance: Assess the potential impact of a

security breach on each system, prioritizing those that handle sensitive data or perform critical functions.

Exposure Risk: Consider the likelihood of a successful attack, factoring in the system's network visibility, firewall protections, and the services it provides that might be vulnerable to exploitation.

Operational Criticality: Determine the system's importance to ongoing business operations, with a special emphasis on systems whose unavailability would significantly disrupt business processes.

While some organizations opt to scan all their systems regularly—a sound practice—it does not negate the necessity for a detailed asset inventory and prioritization. This comprehensive approach is essential not just for scanning but also for efficiently directing remediation efforts based on the criticality and vulnerability of assets. Even if the intent is to scan everything, knowing the significance and potential vulnerabilities of each asset is crucial for tailoring your vulnerability management strategy.

SCANNING PROCESS

Vulnerability scans vary significantly, even when testing identical systems with the same tools, due to numerous influencing factors. A crucial factor is the scan's perspective, heavily dependent on the scanner's network location relative to the target systems. Consider a standard network setup with a firewall, a DMZ hosting a publicly accessible web server, and the internal network. The scan results differ based on where the scanner is placed within this architecture.

If the scanner is within the DMZ, it enjoys direct, unfettered access to the web server, bypassing firewall constraints. This setup unveils the most comprehensive set of vulnerabilities on the server. Conversely, positioning the scanner within the internal network changes the dynamics as its traffic must navigate through the firewall to reach the web server. The firewall may block or filter out certain probes, potentially masking vulnerabilities visible from the DMZ position.

Placing the scanner externally, in the broader internet, offers a view akin to that of an external attacker, subjected to stringent inbound traffic rules applied by the firewall. This perspective might reveal fewer vulnerabilities but is invaluable for understanding what an external threat might exploit, aiding in prioritizing fixes for exposed vulnerabilities.

Each scanning perspective has its merit, providing valuable insights from different angles. A DMZ-based scan uncovers the full range of potential issues, while an internet-based scan highlights vulnerabilities visible to external threats, helping prioritize critical fixes.

Furthermore, firewalls and intrusion prevention systems (IPS) play a pivotal role in shaping scan results by filtering or blocking the scanner's probes based on configured rules and policies. Traditional server-based scanning involves the scanner reaching out to the target system across the network. However, agent-based and credentialed scans offer alternative insights.

Agent-based scanning involves deploying a security agent on each server, which conducts in-depth checks and reports findings to the central management system. While providing deep visibility, this method might be less favored due to its operational complexity.

Credentialed scanning, on the other hand, allows the scanner to log into the system using provided credentials to gather detailed configuration data. This method strikes a balance between deep insights and operational simplicity. For example, configuring Nessus for credentialed scanning involves specifying the type of credentials (SSH or Windows) and providing the necessary authentication details, aiming for read-only access to avoid administrative risks.

In crafting a vulnerability scanning strategy, incorporating various perspectives—server-based, agent-based, and credentialed—ensures a thorough and nuanced understanding of your network's security posture, facilitating a well-rounded defense mechanism.

SCAP PROTOCOL

The effectiveness and outcomes of vulnerability scans can drastically differ, not only based on the tools and systems being examined but also due to several crucial variables. Among these, the location of the vulnerability scanner in relation to the targeted systems within the network architecture plays a fundamental role. Imagine a typical network arrangement featuring a firewall, a Demilitarized Zone (DMZ) with a web server accessible to the public, and the internal network. The placement of the scanner significantly influences the visibility of vulnerabilities.

A scanner located in the DMZ directly interacts with the web server without the limitations imposed by the firewall, potentially revealing a broader spectrum of vulnerabilities. In contrast, a scanner positioned within the internal network must contend with firewall restrictions, which could obscure certain vulnerabilities that would otherwise be detected from a DMZ standpoint.

When the scanner operates from an external position, akin to an external threat actor's perspective, it's subjected to the firewall's stringent rules governing inbound traffic. This positioning might uncover fewer vulnerabilities but is critical for identifying which vulnerabilities are visible to external threats, assisting in the prioritization of remediation efforts.

Each perspective offers unique insights. Scans from the DMZ can unearth a complete array of potential security issues, whereas scans from the external viewpoint prioritize vulnerabilities that are immediately exploitable from outside, guiding the urgency of fixes.

The configuration of firewalls and Intrusion Prevention Systems (IPS) further affects the scan outcomes by filtering or blocking the scanner's attempts based on predefined security policies. Traditional server-based scanning processes involve the scanner probing the target system across the network. However, the deployment of agent-based and credentialed scans provides alternative avenues for discovering vulnerabilities.

Agent-based scanning entails installing a security agent on servers to perform detailed examinations and relay the findings back to a central management platform. Despite offering profound insights, this method might be cumbersome due to the added complexity of managing the agents.

On the flip side, credentialed scanning permits the scanner to authenticate into systems with specified credentials to extract comprehensive configuration details, striking a balance between depth of insight and ease of deployment. Configuring such scans, as seen in tools like Nessus, involves detailing the credential types (SSH or Windows) and authentication specifics, ideally ensuring read-only access to mitigate the risk of unauthorized changes.

By integrating diverse scanning methodologies—server-based, agent-based, and credentialed—organizations can develop a multifaceted understanding of their network's security stance, laying the groundwork for a robust defense strategy.

CVSS (COMMON VULNERABILITY SCORING SYSTEM)

The Common Vulnerability Scoring System (CVSS) is a standardized framework used to rate the severity of security vulnerabilities, presenting each with a score out of ten. This score is derived by evaluating eight distinct metrics that assess various aspects of the vulnerability. Here's a breakdown of these metrics and how they contribute to determining a vulnerability's CVSS score:

- Attack Vector (AV): This metric outlines the means

through which a vulnerability can be exploited. It ranges from:

- Physical (P): Requires the attacker's physical interaction with the device.
- Local (L): The attacker needs either physical or logical access to the device's console.
- Adjacent Network (A): Requires the attacker to be on the same local network.
- Network (N): The vulnerability can be exploited remotely over the network.

Attack Complexity (AC): This indicates the level of complexity involved in exploiting the vulnerability, categorized as either:

- High (H): Exploitation is difficult and may depend on specific conditions.
- Low (L): The vulnerability is relatively easy to exploit.

Privileges Required (PR): This metric evaluates the level of privileges an attacker must possess before exploiting the vulnerability, marked as:

- High (H): Administrative rights are needed.
- Low (L): Requires basic user privileges.
- None (N): No prior access is needed.

User Interaction (UI): This assesses whether the exploitation of the vulnerability requires action from a legitimate user, either:

- Required (R): Needs user participation.
- None (N): Can be exploited without user involvement.

The first four metrics collectively define how easily a vulnerability can be exploited.

Confidentiality (C): This measures the potential impact on data confidentiality, rated as:

- None (N): No impact.
- Low (L): Partial information disclosure is possible.
- High (H): Complete access to all information is possible.

Integrity (I): This evaluates the impact on data integrity, with potential ratings of:

- None (N): No impact.
- Low (L): Some data could be altered.
- High (H): Complete data compromise is possible.

Availability (A): This looks at the impact on system availability, categorized as:

- None (N): No impact.
- Low (L): Performance degradation.
- High (H): Complete shutdown or inaccessibility of the system.

These three metrics assess the potential impact a vulnerability might have on a system.

Scope (S): This metric determines if a vulnerability's impact extends beyond its initial component, either:

- Changed (C): The vulnerability affects additional components beyond its origin.
- Unchanged (U): Impact is confined to the vulnerable component.

By evaluating these eight metrics, CVSS provides a comprehensive score that helps prioritize vulnerability management efforts based on the potential risk and impact of each identified vulnerability.

SCAN REPORTS

In your role as a cybersecurity analyst, a significant portion of your job will involve dissecting and acting upon vulnerability scan reports. Your tasks range from offering detailed technical insights to engineers, developers, and system administrators for issue resolution to simplifying complex data for business executives and providing an overarching view of risk management to security leaders.

To effectively manage this, focus on five key elements when evaluating scan results:

Vulnerability Severity: How critical is the vulnerability in terms of potential damage?

System Criticality: What is the importance of the impacted systems within your organizational infrastructure?

Data Sensitivity: How crucial or sensitive is the data that could be compromised due to the vulnerability?

Remediation Complexity: What are the challenges involved in addressing the vulnerability?

System Exposure: To what extent is the vulnerable system exposed to potential exploitation?

These criteria are instrumental in prioritizing vulnerabilities for an efficient remediation workflow.

Before moving towards remediation, it's essential to validate the vulnerability's existence and accuracy. This step involves moving beyond the scanner's output to apply your expertise and confirm the vulnerability's presence and its accurate prioritization.

Initially, verify the reported vulnerability's authenticity, as scanners can sometimes report false positives due to imprecise signatures or unrecognized mitigating security controls. Examine the scanner's detailed output, focusing on the interaction between the scanner's input and the system's response, to assess the report's accuracy.

For example, a report indicating a critical flaw in an Ubuntu Linux kernel warrants close inspection. A high CVSS score and alarming language suggest a serious issue. Delving into the output section, which specifies the problematic package, and cross-checking with the system can help validate the report.

False positives, such as a report on a Windows server missing a Mac patch, clearly indicate an error. While some false positives may be straightforward to dismiss, always investigate their origin to maintain report integrity.

Occasionally, known vulnerabilities might be acknowledged but mitigated through compensating controls or risk acceptance. Ensure these exceptions are documented to avoid redundant reporting.

Diligently differentiating between true and false reports before escalating for remediation is crucial to maintaining your credibility. Mistakenly reporting non-issues can erode trust in your assessments, making stakeholders skeptical of your future warnings.

Understand the four possible vulnerability report outcomes:

- True Positive: The vulnerability exists as reported.
- False Positive: The report mistakenly indicates a non-existent vulnerability.
- True Negative: No vulnerabilities are found, and none exist.
- False Negative: The scanner overlooks an actual vulnerability.

Grasping these outcomes helps classify vulnerability findings accurately.

CORRELATION OF RESULTS

After filtering out false positives and acknowledging known exceptions in your vulnerability scans, the next step involves integrating these findings with additional data sources. This multi-faceted approach enriches your analysis and aids in prioritizing vulnerabilities for remediation more effectively.

Consulting Industry Standards and Compliance Requirements

A primary reference should be any applicable industry standards, best practices, or specific regulatory obligations your organization faces. Such guidelines often offer detailed advice on prioritizing certain vulnerabilities. For instance, the PCI DSS provides clear directives on handling vulnerabilities within the cardholder data environment, stipulating that to maintain compliance, no high-level vulnerabilities (CVSS base score of 4.0 or above) should be present in the system components. This kind of precise criterion serves as an invaluable tool for analysts navigating the PCI DSS landscape, offering a straightforward framework for assessing compliance through vulnerability management.

Leveraging Internal Technical Resources

Another critical step is to cross-reference scan results with your organization's existing technical resources. Databases like configuration management systems and log archives can shed light on scan findings, especially in identifying and negating false positives. This internal wealth of information not only aids in validating scan accuracy but also in understanding the context of each vulnerability within your specific environment.

Self-Referential Correlation of Scan Data

It may sound unconventional, but comparing current scan outcomes with historical data from previous scans within your organization can reveal significant patterns and trends. Tools like Tenable's SecurityCenter can visualize these trends, making it easier to spot recurring vulnerability types. Such persistent issues signal a deeper systemic problem that warrants a proactive approach. For instance, a consistent appearance of cross-site scripting vulnerabilities in newly developed web applications suggests a foundational lapse in secure coding practices. Addressing these root causes directly, perhaps through developer training or the implementation of standardized secure coding libraries, can prevent vulnerabilities from arising, aligning with the principle that prevention is superior to cure.

By amalgamating insights from standards, internal data, and historical trends, you can refine your vulnerability management process, moving from merely reactive fixes to a more strategic and preventative cybersecurity posture.

Penetration Testing and Bug Bounty

Penetration testing delves deeper than mere vulnerability assessments by actively simulating cyberattacks on systems to identify exploitable vulnerabilities. While these tests actively engage with the target systems, they're structured to avoid harm, stopping short of causing real damage. The essence of penetration testing lies in mimicking the actions of an adversary to reveal how they could breach defenses in practice.

Prior to embarking on a penetration test, it's crucial to establish clear boundaries with the test's sponsor. This involves defining which systems are fair game and the methods that can be employed. To prevent any misinterpretations, these guidelines are typically documented in a formal "Rules of Engagement" agreement.

Penetration tests vary in their approach based on the level of knowledge testers have about the target environment. In a white-box test, testers have comprehensive knowledge of the system, akin to simulating an attack from someone within the organization.

Conversely, a black-box test places testers in the shoes of an outsider, starting with no knowledge of the system. Grey-box tests strike a balance, offering testers partial knowledge of the system, effectively blending efficiency with the element of surprise.

Following the National Institute of Standards and Technology (NIST) recommendations, penetration tests oscillate between discovery and attack phases. Testers first gather intelligence on potential vulnerabilities through reconnaissance—both by analyzing publicly available information and directly probing systems. Innovative tactics, including the use of drones for identifying unprotected wireless networks, can be part of this phase.

Upon identifying a potential entry point, testers move to the attack phase, aiming to breach the system, escalate their access, and explore the network for further vulnerabilities. This phase often involves lateral movement across the network and may include deploying additional tools for deeper penetration. Techniques such as pivoting—using an initially compromised system as a launchpad to target more secured systems—are key strategies employed by testers to mimic authentic attack paths.

Ensuring the longevity of access, testers might install backdoors for re-entry, a tactic aimed at maintaining access even after initial vulnerabilities are patched. It's important for testers to reverse any changes made during the test, returning systems to their original state.

Given their intensive nature, penetration tests are not routine exercises but are invaluable components of a comprehensive security strategy, offering deep insights into an organization's security posture. While resource-intensive, these tests are vital for assessing the resilience of systems against sophisticated attacks.

Bug bounty programs establish a structured methodology for organizations to invite external security experts to scrutinize their systems under a framework that incentivizes the ethical disclosure of vulnerabilities. Typically, organizations initiate these programs with the support of third-party vendors adept at crafting, launching, and managing such initiatives. The essence of running systems connected to the internet is the constant barrage of probes and attacks they endure. A cursory glance at the activity logs of web servers or firewall systems quickly reveals the relentless attempts at intrusion, with the bulk being automated scans by attackers on the lookout for any weak link.

These programs redirect the energy of potential attackers by offering them a platform to legally and beneficially apply their hacking skills, thereby creating a symbiotic relationship between the organization and the hacker community. This approach not only allows hackers to legally earn from their skillset but also enables organizations to fortify their defenses against future malicious attempts on discovered vulnerabilities.

For instance, in a notable payout, Google rewarded a Chinese security expert with over $100,000 for identifying a significant flaw in Pixel phones in January 2018. The creation and management of bug bounty programs demand a nuanced understanding, often leading organizations to partner with specialized vendors. While tech giants might afford the luxury of an internal bug bounty scheme, most entities opt for vendor collaboration, choosing either a fully managed or a semi-managed service model. The vendor typically oversees the program's framework, offering a platform for vulnerability submission and tracking.

Fully managed services extend to the validation and comprehensive analysis of reported vulnerabilities, offering organizations actionable insights, while semi-managed services transition the analytical responsibilities earlier in the process. Adopting a bug bounty program provides organizations a critical lens on the efficacy of their security measures, proving instrumental in identifying and rectifying previously unnoticed vulnerabilities.

A compelling illustration of such a program's value is the U.S. Department of Defense's "Hack the Army" initiative, which, despite the department's high-security awareness, revealed nearly 150 vulnerabilities through the efforts of 52 authorized testers, distributing around $100,000 in bounties. This outcome underscores the integral role bug bounty programs play in enhancing an organization's security posture, provided they are committed to addressing and amending the vulnerabilities identified through the program.

CONTROLLED EXERCISES

Penetration testing can take on a competitive edge, transforming into exercises where teams of attackers square off against defenders in a structured contest. This method of testing doubles as a vulnerability assessment and a practical training session, enhancing the cybersecurity proficiency and situational awareness of the organization's tech personnel.

In these exercises, participants split into groups identified by color-coded team names. The "Red Team" embodies the attackers, striving to infiltrate the systems within the simulated environment. Oppositely, the "Blue Team" adopts the role of guardians, tasked with fortifying and vigilantly defending these systems against the onslaught, applying real-time defensive strategies. Typically, the Blue Team receives preliminary time to strengthen their defenses prior to the commencement of the Red Team's assault.

Overseeing the event are the "White Team" members, who act as impartial arbitrators and note-takers, ensuring the smooth progression of the exercise and mitigating any potential disruptions to actual operational environments. Though competitively structured, the overarching goal uniting all participants is the fortified cybersecurity posture of their organization.

Post-exercise, it's a standard practice to convene the Red and Blue Teams for a debrief, fostering an exchange of insights and strategies employed during the exercise. This session, often termed "Purple Teaming" — a nod to the blend of Red and Blue Team insights — is pivotal for mutual learning and enhancing collective security acumen.

A favored scenario for these exercises is the "Capture the Flag" format, where the Red Team is tasked with specific objectives like disrupting services or exfiltrating data, while success metrics hinge on the objectives achieved by the attackers versus those thwarted by defenders.

To safeguard against potential harm to live environments, these drills are usually conducted within specially designated test environments, creating a risk-free zone for participants to unleash their skills. This approach not only ensures the safety of production systems but also provides a controlled setting for an enriching learning experience.

OTHER ADVANCED CONCEPTS AND

CONCLUSIONS

THE CYBERCRIME INDUSTRY

Cybercrime's evolution into a highly automated enterprise reflects its transition from mere mischief to a major, lucrative criminal activity. Initially, viruses spread via floppy disks, but as the digital landscape evolved, so did the methods of infection, with USB drives, compromised websites, and email becoming primary vectors. The automation of cybercrime, facilitated by the internet's expansion, allowed it to surpass even drug trafficking in profitability.

At the heart of this automated criminal enterprise is the concept of a botnet, orchestrated by an individual known as a Botmaster. This criminal manages a network of infected computers, or zombies, through command and control servers, often masking their malicious traffic as legitimate to evade detection. These servers, frequently hijacked legitimate websites, are disposable, used briefly before being replaced to avoid capture. Botnets, potentially controlling millions of zombies, are tasked with tasks like data theft, spam distribution, or launching distributed denial-of-service attacks.

Communication between the Botmaster and zombies is maintained using domain generation algorithms, ensuring the network's resilience despite changing command and control points. One of the most infamous botnets, Zeus, exemplifies the sophistication of modern cybercrime. Available as a botnet kit, it enables criminals to customize their attacks, specializing in stealing online credentials through advanced techniques like intercepting browser input or altering bank website interfaces.

The structure of cybercrime mirrors that of a complex, organized business, involving a spectrum of roles from the criminals orchestrating the campaigns to the enablers providing technical support, and the victims. A typical cybercrime operation, such as banking fraud, follows a meticulous process: targeting through surveillance, deploying custom malware, quality assurance testing, delivery via botnets, and finally, the illicit transfer of stolen funds through disposable accounts.

A critical component in the laundering of these funds involves "money mules" – individuals who withdraw stolen money, often under duress or financial strain, risking legal consequences. Recently, a trend toward professional mules offers a more efficient, albeit costly, means of converting digital theft into physical currency, showcasing the sophisticated and organized nature of modern cybercrime.

ADVANCED CONCEPTS: ROOTKITS

Skilled attackers have evolved from using elementary concealing tactics to embedding malware deep within an operating system's core, utilizing what's termed as a rootkit. To plant a rootkit, attackers must first infiltrate the target system. They employ a dropper, which either harbors the rootkit as its payload or fetches it post-breach. The dropper's tasks include verifying the absence of the rootkit on the target, discerning the operational environment, including virtual machine detection and geographical checks. Once it deems the system a viable target, it embeds the rootkit, ensuring its persistence through reboots.

Rootkits are crafted not to exploit but to stealthily function, leveraging standard system operations without self-propagation. They are distinct from viruses, serving as clandestine implants within a host system. However, when fused with virus-like functionalities, rootkits can spread laterally within systems post-installation.

Designed to evade detection mechanisms, rootkits often target disabling antivirus and intrusion detection software. Their ultimate camouflage lies within the operating system's kernel—the central core—where intrusion detection systems' visibility is limited. Gaining kernel access typically involves rootkits being coded as loadable kernel modules or drivers, requiring sophisticated programming capabilities. Such deep integration allows rootkits to operate with the highest system privileges, rendering them nearly undetectable and omnipotent within the host.

A pivotal tactic employed by rootkits is Direct Kernel Object Manipulation (DKOM), manipulating kernel data structures to conceal their presence. An example is altering the EPROCESS list, which tracks active processes, to hide rootkit processes from system monitors like the Task Manager.

Rootkits also establish secure command and control channels, often via encrypted SSH connections, ensuring exclusive access for the attackers while concealing malware downloads from network monitoring tools.

A real-life example of a sophisticated rootkit is the Trojan Downloader 3 (TDL3), developed by the Dogma Millions cybercrime group. TDL3, masquerading as a printer driver to gain kernel privileges, utilizes an encrypted filesystem that expands backwards from the disk's end, rendering it invisible to standard scans. It's designed for varied malicious activities, from keystroke logging to launching distributed denial of service attacks, all while meticulously tracking installations for billing purposes.

A NOTE ON APTs

In recent times, the digital security landscape has seen a stark rise in threats emanating from nation-states employing complex malware, referred to as Advanced Persistent Threats (APTs). APTs, designed to target specific political and military entities, employ a broad spectrum of methods to infiltrate and persist within targets stealthily over extended periods.

APTs distinguish themselves from other malicious software through five primary traits. Firstly, they are intricately tailored to their designated targets, diverging from generic malware models. This specificity enables them to focus their efforts on particular systems or networks. Secondly, they utilize a plethora of sophisticated, sometimes previously unknown (zero-day), exploits to breach defenses. Thirdly, unlike automated malware, APTs often require some level of human oversight for deployment. Once established within a system, they adopt a 'low and slow' strategy, maintaining stealth to avoid detection.

APTs aim to fulfill various objectives that might evolve over time, depending on the attacker's intent. They might be deployed for espionage to pilfer critical information from nation-state targets or to sabotage vital infrastructure systems, such as telecoms, power, or water services, thereby causing significant disruption.

To achieve these ends, APTs incorporate five essential functionalities. Command and control mechanisms allow attackers to steer the malware, download new malicious payloads, or update existing ones. Rather than acting as standalone applications, APTs often latch onto existing processes or applications within memory, a technique called malware injection, to blend in seamlessly. To stay under the radar, considerable effort is invested in developing sophisticated cloaking subsystems, ensuring the malware's actions remain invisible to system administrators.

For data exfiltration, APTs stealthily siphon off targeted information, encrypting and camouflaging it within seemingly benign network traffic, such as HTTP or DNS requests. Additionally, APTs are designed to reactivate upon system reboot or attempts at removal, a feature termed reignition, often using multiple methods to ensure persistence.

A prime example of an APT in action is Stuxnet, a military-grade malware detected in 2010, specifically engineered to disrupt Iranian nuclear centrifuges. It was later revealed that the U.S. and Israel were behind its creation. Stuxnet showcased the capability to spread via email, USB drives, or pre-compromised equipment, targeting isolated systems not directly connected to the internet. Utilizing unknown Windows vulnerabilities for propagation, it ultimately manipulated the Siemens SCADA control software to damage the centrifuges physically.

The discovery of APTs usually occurs when anomalous network activity, such as attempts to connect to command and control servers, is detected. Defense against APTs poses a significant challenge, with detection often delayed for months post-infiltration. As such, advanced persistent threats represent a sophisticated and enduring category of malware, signaling a continuous threat in the evolving cyber warfare arena.

NIST FRAMEWORK

At the Third Global Conference on Cyberspace in Seoul in 2013, nations worldwide acknowledged the critical importance of cybersecurity in the Seoul framework, underscoring the internet's role in fostering growth and the shared responsibility in securing cyberspace. Following this, in 2014, the U.S. National Institute of Standards and Technology (NIST) introduced the Framework for Improving Critical Infrastructure Cybersecurity, which has since emerged as a leading standard in the field.

he NIST Cybersecurity Framework adopts a proactive stance on security with three main components: the Framework Core,

Framework Profile, and Framework Implementation Tiers. The Core of the framework outlines fundamental cybersecurity activities across five functions: Identify, Protect, Detect, Respond, and Recover. These functions are further broken down into 23 categories that cover various security tasks. For instance, within the Detect function, categories include anomalies and events, security continuous monitoring, and detection processes. Diving deeper, categories are divided into more specific controls. For example, detection processes involve aspects such as defining roles and responsibilities, adherence to legal requirements, evaluation of detection processes, sharing of detection insights, and fostering continual enhancement.

Rather than proposing new security measures, the NIST Cybersecurity Framework organizes existing best practices into a structured format. It references established control standards such as COBIT, ISA/IEC 62443, ISO 27000 series, and NIST's own SP 800-53, providing organizations with a roadmap to craft a modern cybersecurity posture that leverages well-regarded industry standards.

The Framework Profile stands as the second element within the NIST Cybersecurity Framework, acting as a strategic bridge that links cybersecurity practices with business objectives, offering insights into risk management and guiding plans to enhance alignment. The Framework culminates with a structured approach to assessing cybersecurity maturity through Implementation Tiers.

Starting at the foundational tier, "Partial," cybersecurity practices may seem sporadic and reactive, with risk management efforts not systematically driven by organizational risk objectives or outcomes, and external collaboration on cybersecurity issues is minimal. Progressing to the "Risk Informed" tier, risk management practices become more organized, though not consistently applied throughout the organization, and information sharing about cybersecurity remains largely internal.

The "Repeatable" tier marks a point where risk management protocols are both formalized into policies and responsive to evolving risk landscapes, supported by active internal and external communication. The pinnacle, "Adaptive," represents a highly dynamic approach where organizations proactively and flexibly adjust their cybersecurity measures in response to new threats, vulnerabilities, and changes in their digital environment.

NIST advises that organizations adopt a dual-profile strategy within the Cybersecurity Framework. The initial profile should accurately reflect the organization's current cybersecurity stance, based on selected activities deemed essential. This serves as a baseline for current security measures. The secondary profile outlines the desired, or target, state of cybersecurity, establishing an acceptable risk threshold tailored to specific organizational needs. This framework allows for a structured action plan aimed at bridging the gap between the current and targeted cybersecurity postures.

For organizations initiating their cybersecurity framework, key steps include pinpointing critical business outcomes, comprehending associated threats and vulnerabilities, crafting an initial profile, conducting thorough risk assessments, setting a goal for the desired cybersecurity state, identifying and prioritizing discrepancies to develop a strategic action plan, and diligently executing said plan to bolster cybersecurity defenses.

COVIT FRAMEWORK

COBIT, standing for Control Objectives for Information and Related Technology, is a prominent framework developed by the Information Systems Audit and Control Association (ISACA). Its core aim is to provide organizations with a robust, auditable governance and management structure for IT, which in turn generates value for stakeholders. COBIT's structure is predicated on a series of processes categorized into four primary domains: planning, building, delivering, and monitoring.

The planning domain, known fully as Align, Plan and Organize, contains 14 distinct processes aimed at alignment and organization. The building domain, termed Build, Acquire, and Implement, involves 11 processes focused on development and implementation.

The delivery domain, Deliver, Service and Support, comprises six processes dedicated to the provision of services. Lastly, the monitoring domain, Monitor, Evaluate and Assess, includes four processes aimed at oversight and evaluation.

Predominantly utilized within the financial sector for IT controls audits, aligning with COBIT helps organizations meet regulatory requirements effectively. Within the realm of cybersecurity, two processes stand paramount: APO13, which addresses overall management of security within the planning phase, and DSS05, focused on the management of security services during delivery. However, security is a cross-cutting theme impacting numerous other processes, such as incident management found under DSS02, Manage Service Requests and Incidents.

Delving into APO13, Managed Security, we find it encompasses defining, operating, and monitoring an information security management framework aimed at five key objectives: ensuring compliance, managing IT and enterprise risk, enhancing IT cost transparency, safeguarding information and infrastructure, and underpinning decision-making with reliable data. APO13 articulates through three control objectives, focusing on establishing an Information Security Management System (ISMS), devising and managing a security plan to achieve desired security levels, and ongoing monitoring and review of the ISMS. Implementing APO13 often involves adopting a suite of controls from ISO 27001, setting standards for information security management systems, thereby ensuring a comprehensive approach to information security.

INCIDENT MANAGEMENT

I n an era where cybercrime and state-sponsored cyber activities are intensifying, it's a matter of when, not if, an organization will face an attack. The true test lies in the organization's readiness to handle such incidents. The NIST Cybersecurity Framework lays out control objectives under the "Respond" function, encompassing five key areas: preparation, communication, analysis, mitigation, and post-event activities. Additionally, the framework's "Recovery" function complements the response process, enhancing the organization's ability to bounce back post-incident.

These categories echo the incident response phases detailed in NIST's SP 800-61 Incident Handling Guide, albeit with a slight structural difference in terms of communication flow. Aligning with international standards, the NIST framework and the SP 800-61 are also in sync with CREST UK's tri-phase model, emphasizing preparation, action, and post-action steps in incident management.

A pivotal element of effective incident response is the exchange and sharing of information, crucial for both the anticipatory stage and during the heat of an incident. Established by NIST in 1990, the Forum of Incident Response and Security Teams (FIRST) supports this need, facilitating workshops, conferences, and a platform for incident response professionals to collaborate and share insights globally.

National Computer Incident Response Teams (CIRTS) play a vital role at the country level, safeguarding government operations and critical infrastructure while offering cybersecurity guidance to the public. Entities like the US CERT within the Department of Homeland Security exemplify this, acting as a hub for incident coordination and information dissemination on cybersecurity threats and vulnerabilities.

International cooperation is furthered through forums like FIRST, which not only promote national CIRT collaboration but also engage in training and global cybersecurity discourse. Standardizing incident communication with a universally understood classification system is beneficial. The US CERT delineates seven incident categories, ranging from unauthorized access (Category 1) to investigations of anomalous activity (Category 6).

Incident classification isn't always straightforward. Initial indicators may necessitate further scrutiny before they can be accurately categorized. Essential to the incident management process is the Trouble Ticket System, a repository for tracking incident details from initial detection through to resolution. An example of such a system is OS Ticket, which organizes and displays ongoing incident tickets for efficient handling.

ATTACK DETECTION

Exploring the stages of operational response in incident management involves the NIST framework, which outlines detection and analysis, containment, eradication, recovery, and post-incident activities. The initial phase, detection and analysis, is an ongoing effort to identify signs of a cyber intrusion, a task typically performed by a Security Operations Center (SOC) analyst. This phase focuses on identifying potential external threats and the presence of malware within the organization, monitoring outgoing signals to command and control servers, and observing internal movements indicative of a breach expanding within the network.

Tools like Splunk, Graylog, and ELK Stack are utilized by SOC analysts to sift through log data and trigger alerts based on predefined criteria. The demanding nature of this role requires continuous vigilance over streams of data to discern potential security incidents from regular IT hiccups, a process that often relies as much on an analyst's instinct as on the intelligence provided by these systems.

Identifying genuine cyber threats is complicated by the high frequency of false positives from sources like Intrusion Detection Systems (IDS). Analysts must strike a balance between underreacting, which could allow a threat to materialize, and overreacting, which risks alarm fatigue. Once a security event is verified, the complexity of its symptoms demands a nuanced analysis to understand the breach's nature, scope, and severity.

Incidents are signaled by precursors, hints of potential future attacks like reconnaissance activities, or indicators, which suggest an ongoing or occurred breach, such as unusual outbound traffic patterns. Distinguishing between false alarms and genuine threats is crucial, with a thorough understanding of normal network behaviors serving as a key differentiator. Reference to a knowledge base can expedite this process by identifying previously encountered anomalies.

Monitoring tools provide visibility into network traffic, helping analysts spot abnormal data movements or unexpected activity on usually quiet ports. Advanced analytics and deep packet inspection contribute to detecting sophisticated threats like APTs by offering detailed insights over time.

Transitioning from detection to declaring an official incident necessitates careful prioritization. Incidents are not merely queued for attention in the order they appear but are evaluated and addressed based on their potential impact on business operations, ensuring critical threats are managed with the urgency they require.

THE JOURNEY AHEAD IN CYBERSECURITY

As we close this guide on cybersecurity for beginners, it's essential to recognize that the landscape of digital security is ever-evolving. The principles, practices, and tools we've discussed are foundational, but they are just the beginning of a much larger journey. Cybersecurity is not a destination but a continuous process of learning, adapting, and vigilance.

The world of technology advances at a breakneck pace, and with each new development, new vulnerabilities emerge. As beginners, you have taken the first step into a field that is critical not just to the functioning of our digital infrastructure but to the preservation of our privacy and the protection of our personal and professional lives.

Embracing a Culture of Security

One of the most important takeaways from this book should be the mindset of security. Cybersecurity isn't solely the responsibility of IT professionals; it's a culture that needs to be embraced by everyone who interacts with digital devices and the internet. This means staying informed about the latest threats, understanding the basics of secure behavior online, and always questioning the security of the systems and services you use.

Lifelong Learning

In cybersecurity, the learning never stops. What is considered secure today may be vulnerable tomorrow. Therefore, commitment to ongoing education is crucial. This could mean formal education, such as courses or certifications, or informal learning, such as following cybersecurity news, participating in online forums, and experimenting with new technologies in a safe and controlled environment.

Engaging with the Community

The cybersecurity community is vast and welcoming, full of professionals and enthusiasts who share a common goal: to make the digital world a safer place. Engaging with this community can provide you with invaluable insights, mentorship, and updates on the latest in cybersecurity trends and threats. Conferences, webinars, online forums, and local meet-up groups are great ways to connect with others on the same path.

Ethical Considerations

As you grow in your cybersecurity career or interest, remember the importance of ethics. The skills you develop have the power to protect or harm, and it is imperative to use them responsibly. Upholding ethical standards is not just about personal integrity; it's about contributing to the trust and security that form the backbone of our digital society.

The Future of Cybersecurity

Looking forward, the challenges in cybersecurity will only grow as technology becomes increasingly integrated into every aspect of our lives. Artificial intelligence, the Internet of Things, quantum computing, and other emerging technologies will bring both advancements and new vulnerabilities. As a beginner, you now have the foundation to contribute to this field, whether as a professional, an informed citizen, or both.

Conclusion

This book has equipped you with the knowledge to understand the basics of cybersecurity, but it is the curiosity, vigilance, and commitment to continuous learning and ethical practice that will define your journey from here. The path ahead is challenging but rewarding, filled with opportunities to protect, discover, and innovate. Welcome to the world of cybersecurity, where your contributions can make a real difference in safeguarding our digital future.

ABOUT THE AUTHOR

Maria Bryght is a seasoned IT consultant, educator, and author with over two decades of experience in the technology industry. Maria has dedicated her career to advancing IT practices, cybersecurity, and Identity and Access Management (IAM) strategies across various sectors. Her contributions to the field are also captured in her writing. She is the author of several influential books on cybersecurity and IT in general, recognized for their clarity, depth, and practical guidance.

www.ingramcontent.com/pod-product-compliance
Lightning Source LLC
Chambersburg PA
CBHW052140070326
40690CB00047B/1327